D1521616

Boys will be boys

The University of Chicago Press / Chicago and London

BOYS WILL BE BOYS

a daughter's elegy

{SARA SULERI GOODYEAR}

Sara Suleri Goodyear is professor of English at Yale
University. Writing as Sara Suleri, she is the author
of *The Rhetoric of English India* and of the acclaimed
memoir *Meatless Days,* both published by the
University of Chicago Press.

Affectionate thanks to Professor Muhammad Umar
Memon for his help with the calligraphy.

The University of Chicago Press, Chicago 60637
The University of Chicago Press, Ltd., London
© 2003 by The University of Chicago
All rights reserved. Published 2003
Printed in the United States of America

12 11 10 09 08 07 06 05 04 03   1 2 3 4 5
ISBN: 0-226-30401-9 (cloth)

Library of Congress Cataloging-in-Publication Data

Goodyear, Sara Suleri.
    Boys will be boys : a daughter's elegy / Sara Suleri
Goodyear.
        p.   cm.
    ISBN 0-226-30401-9 (alk. paper)
    1. Suleri, Z. A. (Ziauddin Ahmad), 1913–1999.
    2. Journalists—Pakistan—Biography.   3. Goodyear,
Sara Suleri,   I. Title.
    PN5449.P18Z743   2003
    070.92—dc21
    [B]   2003051352

♾ The paper used in this publication meets the
minimum requirements of the American National
Standard for Information Sciences—Permanence of
Paper for Printed Library Materials, ANSI Z39.48-1992.

For Austin

For Shahid, Tillat, Irfan

Contents

Boys will be boys

It was several years ago—decades, I imagine—that my sisters and I decided that each of us would always wear the same perfume. Not precisely the same, that is, but whatever we happened to be wearing at the moment, so that over the continental drift that we spread ourselves, there would be a way of allaying that aching distance. As an idea of frivolity it worked quite well: amidst the habitual absence that was our wont, we could indeed pick up a garment and say, "Yes, this is a Nuzhat smell, this is an Ifat smell, this is a Sara smell, this is a Tillat smell." And thus the delicacy of absence itself could be made as concrete as a fabric. We must have come to this decision on some summer afternoon in Lahore, which spread its solitude around us. I said yes to my sisters, what a jolly idea, how I would love to pick up a sock or a frock or a scarf and make of those items the touch of my desire. There is no question that

2

we sisters were often in agreement, but on the subject of perfume, I believe they cheated. When we met, they emanated the most suspicious odors. So I can never be certain that they indeed kept their promises, although I, in a certain sullen gesture of fidelity—for what is fidelity but habit?—have.

I think I must have been in a similar mood of extravagance when I concluded that each of them should be conferred with the middle initial of "S" when I addressed envelopes to them with their married names. For I still wrote letters in those days, a trick that has curiously left my life. The "S" was meant to signify "soul," or "sister," or something equally sentimental: Ifat and Tillat simply laughed and shrugged it away, but Nuz, with the tenacity of the literally faithful, saw through my lie. After my sorry gift of an initial, she never wrote to me or any one of us without asserting a different nomenclature. In her charming, sprawling handwriting, she would put my name upon an envelope and then declare the sender's name to be Nuzhat Suleri Akhund. If not scent, in other words, there could be Suleri. It made me shy at first, but when I remarked upon her new name to my father, he looked up with a near-gratitude for his firstborn and said, "I know."

Yes, Pip, you knew. I must have as well, when you trudged up the bitter stairs into the room of Nuzzi's death and turned to me—angry and weary—to utter, "She should have been making this trip for me." "*Of course* she should have," I responded with bravado. "What earthly use are you at this age?" And that exchange gave a further comradeship to our conception of what the secrecy of tears may be. She gone so suddenly and you so perplexed. But then came another gesture toward her absence: "Where do you think she is?" you asked me, startlingly. I mused about how that question would have moved Nuz to a perplexed laughter, just as the time when our brother Shahid strode into her morning bedroom in Karachi and seized her mattress, joggling it violently, in order to make a boisterous greeting to his nephew. Instead, he found our astonished and dear brother-in-law Feroze wondering why he should have been awakened in such an extraordinary fashion. I cannot remember why Shahid and I were together in Karachi at that time. It could not have been for Nuzzi's funeral.

But it certainly was that era, after Pip had left Karachi, when we children were invited to his dear friend's for luncheon. Dr. Sadiq was proud of his extremely hospitable and welcoming board: "No, no, we do not want to go," wailed Tillat and I to our brothers. "I'll take care of it," said Shahid with levity, with gravity. And so we went. Our imaginations had been modest: at lunchtime, surely not a time to engage in much consumption, who would consider quails, baby chickens, rice, and much palaver as bare necessities? I have omitted to mention the peacock eggs. But certainly Shahid performed his task: while I was sorrowfully whispering "miaow" to a cage of extremely noisy canaries in the Sadiqs' courtyard, my brother had got to work. The daughters-in-law who were serving us sat back in speechless admiration as Shahid yelled, "*Bater*, quails, give me two! If not two, then four!" Then he sang with great energy, "The animals came in two by two, *vive la compagnie!*"

He allowed us to eat noiselessly and nothing, while our hostesses were consumed by his voracious manner and practice of discourse. By the time the third course arrived, Shahid was singing, "One more river, and that's the river of Jordan, one more river, and that's the river to cross!" When, in exhausted conclusion, he was offered some Kashmiri tea—a pink beverage, more milk than tea—he exclaimed, "No, no! Pink is for girls!" But then his equanimity returned. After the groaning board had been dismantled, he clutched his head in a low moan. Sadiq's daughters-in-law were alarmed: "What is it, Shahid, what is it?" they asked. He looked up with something close to despair. "I forgot to eat the lentils," he replied.

But as we know, food can be cruel and unusual. In Rawalpindi summertimes, it was our ritual to travel to the mountains: even for a day, if not a month. Mamma was in England and Pip was missing her, when he decided that we should take a day trip to Nathia Gali and have a picnic in the hills. Pip's idea of such a trip is as follows: no strenuous walks in the brisk mountain air, oh, no, but a comfortable carpet spread out upon a grassy knoll that commanded a beautiful view, and a cigar. In preparation, I was in charge of the accoutrements, and Tillat in charge of ordering lunch. Poor Tillat. When we were up in the hills and the picnic was being spread out, Papa looked suspiciously at the sight of one roast chicken, delectable, but small. There were four of us to eat. "Tillat," he asked, "what were you thinking of?" Tillat: "Well, if each of us had a leg, along with everything else, we should just be fine!" Pip, with astonishment: "Tillat, how many legs does a chicken have?" And my Tillat, in some combination of defiance and defensiveness, answered: "Four." The winds and their heady conifer fragrance whipped around us; little monkeys sat on the pines in the hopes we would leave something uneaten; and my father simply stared at my sister, repeating: "How many legs does a chicken have?—four." She has not been allowed to forget that story.

Years later, she had her own consumption tale. It was during the Gulf War when luckily she and her family had left Kuwait for a holiday in the Cotswolds. I rang to tell her about the invasion, but she was sleepy and cross. "Sara, how you exaggerate!" she said, and I wished I could be proven wrong. So there they were, marooned in London. And then Pip arrived too, for some cornea operation on his beautiful eyes, which never recovered. And here, I must give credit to my sister's stamina. She, disrupted from her home, in a little rented house in London, her husband Farooq in Pakistan, then a recuperating Pip in the loving but constant care of Shahid, and *then* a visit from me! What confusion! She made some definite rules. "There can be no smoking in this house," she said unequivocally, "and no drinking either!" (Tillat is the best Mozzi among us; if she doesn't raise her index finger to do Ashadoana La Illah ha Illalah five times a day, at least she does it twice.) Shahid and I concurred generously and proceeded to move ourselves into her little garage that overlooked an extremely rainy driveway. We found an ashtray, Shahid set up a little bar, and gradually all the family seemed to converge into that nook. It was there that Pip, musing on his cigar, began to descant about translation. I had made the mistake of telling him about my attempted translation of Ghālib and how perplexed I was at trying to recast the line

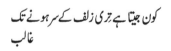

I am still unable to do that today. How stupid and clumsy it seems to say, "Who lives, until your hair can reach its head"? In any case, we were musing, under those cramped circumstances, and Pip, who loved Ghālib with a passion typical to his nature, suddenly exclaimed to me, "Essence!" And then he held forth. "Translation is not in the word; it is the essence!" I stared at the English rain and listened for what seemed like the longest time, until Shahid came to my rescue. "Pip," he said, "remember that song"

بَجَّن، جھوٹ مَت بولو

خُدا کے پاس جانا ہے

نہ ہاتھی ہے، نہ گھوڑا ہے

وہاں پیدل ہی جانا ہے!

Pip was too dignified to recall. But my brother persisted. "In the shower this morning, *here* is what I came up with!"

"Darling, darling, do not lie,
Sooner later we all die,
We don't go there in coat and pant,
We don't go there on elephant!

"Now, Pip, don't you think I've extracted the essence? The essence, Pip, the essence in *elephant*!" My father tried not to look amused, but he was and turned his huge voice to me instead to quote more of Ghālib.

We always read to one another. On my last visit to Lahore—the last time I saw you, Pip—you were barely back from the hospital and each of us knew that you were dying, not even able to move your lion's head with its old impetuous manner. Then, in those early Lahore mornings— a scented light, irreplaceable—I would clamber into your bed to prop you up, back to back, and read you the headlines, the *surkhi*s, for news- papers still arrived inordinately, although you could not read. I would read *surkhi* after *surkhi*, and then pray inside me that you would not need to hear the following article. Sometimes you did. I hate to admit it, but reading English was easier for me, and when you asked for an article in Urdu, I felt incompetent beyond belief. Those Urdu newspapers, with their tiny print and ink leaking all over your fingers (not that your English ones were any better, Pip), how hard I had to concentrate! And you'd shame me, as I spelled out with the diligence of an eight-year-old "bubble-o-nihar": "Lail-oh Nihar," you'd quietly say with an inadvertent wince, still seeking to be kind to me. But we would be overtaken by my stepsister, running into the bedroom to thrust boiled eggs into your mouth. Never a great believer in eggs of that sort, it made me squeamish. In retrospect, I can definitely say that boiled eggs interfered too much in the last days of your life.

Oh, yes, newspapers and governments could come and go in Pakistan, but then there was always Pip. He didn't understand or enjoy my amusement when General Zulu Haq took the helm and announced to some bewildered foreign journalists, "We are hodgepodge." Smilingly, he said it. "Pakistan is hodgepodge." In other words, who cares for constitutions when Pakistan is perfectly happy separating its hodge from its podge? I cannot say I wept when, some years later, an aerial explosion caused General Zulu in his patriotic generosity to spread himself over Bahawalpur, never the most arable of Pakistani terrains. Pip also was not particularly taken by my demeanor a few years prior, when, accompanying him to the Oval Office, I watched Zulu and Carter shake hands. "I know you are a very religious man," said Carter, and continued to shake his hand. They were peas in a pod, size-wise, despite the distance of race between them. Everyone was smiling at that prolonged handshake; I tried not to look too tall until my sobriety failed, and I burst into a clatter of laughter. "How could you be so effusive?" Pip chided, when we returned to the peace of our hotel rooms.

But this is not a story of governments, or else we would have to retreat into the Benazir Bhutto era, the Bobby Shafto—Nawaz Sharif—era, and then enter into the present times that Pip cannot see. The first Benazir era promised some hope, until she married her scoundrel. Nuz made me happy on the latter score by mailing to me in New Haven an epithalamion for our head of state published in a Karachi newspaper. It contained the inimitable lines:

Apron strings?—Never! Plenty to match her!
Indira Gandhi and Margaret Thatcher!

And Bobby Shafto, fat and fair, with his Model Town estates and innumerable mills of corruption, what harm was it for him to go to jail? What a surprise, then, when the current regime (I am telling you this, Pip, because I know you would be interested) let him loose and banished him to Saudi Arabia! As Shahid profoundly commented, "I would far rather live in the Attock jail—with that charming view—than sit in a Riyadh palace with Idi Amin as my chum!" We watched the governments as, in my childhood, we watched the jails of which Pip was in and out. I was never allowed to visit him there, which strikes me as peculiar, because we were routinely taken to visit friends and family in hospitals, and they are surely the more detestable spaces. But Pip certainly knew—solitary and brooding—how to hate confinement.

He built a would-be garden for himself in the tiny patch outside his cell, this time at the Lahore jail. My mother must have taken him the seeds, the saplings, for no one knew how long the Gurmani case would run. It was a government, a sedition, matter, but the guards came and tore down Pip's garden. He later told me that it was not the bars that broke his heart but the sight of his zinnias, his photolax, being trampled into the ground with an indifferent trudge. Of course he was not allowed pen and paper, for fear that he might produce another fiery article, not books either, for fear that he might rest. And so he planted flowers instead, an eye upon that little tent of blue that prisoners call the sky. And when they tore the garden up, his heart broke, for Pip was never a patient man.

If there is one thing that I most miss from Pakistan, it has to be the *mali*, the gardeners of a most vanishing breed. They always looked wise, in some inexplicable fashion, and spoke slowly, with deliberation. Here were us women trying to suggest what to plant in some festive flower bed and the gardener—I have forgotten his name; it doesn't matter—took notes as though he were inscribing the Bible. "Ball-sum," he said, writing out each syllable, "too-lips," "holy-hock!" Sweet peas were something like "freak-pee," but I am too modest to elaborate on that further.

And yet there they were, cascades of flowers, with the gardener—always surly—making his daily rounds. He must have picked up those tiny little shrubs from the nurseries that used to line the canal in Lahore, emitting such wonderful fragrances. I am not sure that the nurseries are still there, for I have not returned in years.

It seems decades ago when Nuz and I, driving through Clifton in Karachi, chose to stop at the Abdullah Shah Ghazi shrine. We did not really want the shrine, you see; we wanted the *totas*. Those parrots and those parrot mongers were all we needed: we certainly did not need to climb those monstrous stairs to see what the saint could proffer. Nuzzi's friend—in a gesture of kind generosity—had lent us a car and driver for the day, and so we went off in considerable merriment. We went first to Jinnah's tomb, a hideous edifice monumentalizing Quaid-e-Azam, the Father of the Nation, and remembering Pip's devotion to the man, we called it "Quaidy-Daddy." And then we were off to the shrine. The driver could not understand what we meant when Nuz muttered to him, with some embarrassment, "*Totas.*" In other words, we were not to enter the shrine, but to squat instead next to the fortune-telling parrots, on a most unlovely pavement. And it was entrancing. The parrot, at the command of the parrot monger, would shuffle up and read your palm: then, quite succinctly and deftly, it would walk to the cards laid along that dusty pavement and pick one up. Then you could read your fortune. Nuzzi's fortune card was somewhat troublesome, for it told her: "You are a very bad woman. Mend your ways, or else begone!" "That's *your* fortune, Sara," Nuz said to me with irritation. "It can't possibly be mine!" But the parrot walked on, beaked another card, and handed it to me. I cannot describe my consternation, my concern, when I read upon it: "Guide yourself accordingly."

It was too dark for me to fathom, amidst an oppressive Karachi sunlight, but I think I did take it back with me, the parrot and its message. In the days when you were put into the grave, Pip, I was in a puzzled wonderment. Then, when beloved Eqbal Ahmad—to die himself just weeks later—sent me a sheaf of your obituaries, I could not read, I could not even look. It behooved me to give them to Irfan, my baby brother, when I was next in England. And with what laughter he emerged onto the porch where we were sitting, to tell us that one of the obituaries declared that Z. A. Suleri was a keen admirer of *Kabbaddi*—a terrible game, played in the Punjab, and certainly not a favorite of my father's, I promise you.

"*Kodi, kodi,*" I said—an inexplicable refrain of that game—and took it into my bosom. You would have humor enough to live with it, my Pip, even with the country dismantling around you. You did try, didn't you, to keep it whole and sole? So what else can I say when Eqbal's obituaries reached me, and I had to face your death mask on a page? My fingers were inky, damp, as they realized the true tragedy of newsprint. And then the whisper was

لازم تھا کہ دیکھو مرا رستہ کوئی دن اور
تنہا گئے کیوں؟ اب رہو تنہا کوئی دن اور
غالب

But our paths had to cross again some other day.
Going alone, now stay alone until some other day.

— G H Ā L I B

عاشقی صَبر طلب ...
غالب

Love demands patience

— G H Ā L I B

𝒩ewsprint, begone. I really do not wish to wonder what you did and did not do to my father's life. After all, he loved newsprint, so who am I to set up vociferous complaint against its texture? Or even consider why he could regard it as the most tangible form of history that he could hold in his life? For some curious reason, Mamma knew, in all the ways she apprehended both her husband and her children. My mother in the Second World War worked in the Admiralty with someone called Arthur Bryant and went—little Fabian that she was—to an evening lecture on the independence of India. There she saw my father talk, and doubtless he was eloquent. He was to his dying day. That is part of the reason he

got his name: Patriotic and Preposterous equals Pip. There he is in a nut-
shell, counting himself king of infinite space, except that he never told us
his bad dreams. But Mamma knew. Why else would she have turned in
1945 to a friend attending the same lecture to say, "Now, I could marry
that man"? And then she did. Great war was in the air at the time of
their marriage, with London heart-strung: there were air raids, blackouts,
blitzes, rations. But that unlikely pair still chose to get married.

I have heard her stories about the war and what it entailed, so that
years later when Pakistan and India went to war in 1965—as is their foolish habit—I stole down to the basement of our house. I put there a bottle of desiccated coconut and an apple so that if we were marooned,
we would have at least a jot of sustenance. How my siblings shrieked
with laughter when I confessed to my heroic war effort. "What if we
were bombed and stuck in the basement? Are you the one who would
dole out rations of desiccated coconut?" Of course I was embarrassed,
but the war was real. With Lahore barely seventeen miles from the border, we had no choice but to hear that petrifying music. And then during this shortest war, with patriotic songs blaring around us, we drove
into the city, toward the Ravi River. There I saw the prisoners, manacled,
fresh from the front, being paraded on the streets of Lahore. There were
Sikh soldiers being forced to walk along the paths of an ancient city
where their founding saint, Gurū Nānak, could be buried. Aside from
the shame we felt when we saw those men, my child's eye said to itself,
"So that's what faces look like when they are in despair."

Mamma loved the Ravi and the Old City. I could not imagine how
her Welsh blood could have taken it, not just the Anārkalī bazaar, but
the old city itself, its tiny lanes and crowded commerce, and its breathtaking gates. Pip never went to the Old City: maybe he was too familiar
with such getting and spending, with all his years in Delhi. But Mam
came, certainly not as a tourist, but as a woman who loved to see those
stalls full of garlands, the red roses and the easily bruised white *motia*,
smelling so sweet, and smelling so sour. And at the heart of the Old City,
the sudden ravishment of the Wazir Khan Mosque: I went there several
times with different friends. When I was with David, an old artisan at the
mosque asked him, "And what religion do you belong to?" David, my

Jewish partner, replied—in tender carefulness—"I am in quest." That satisfied the artisan considerably. "Quest," he nodded, "quest. That is an honorable place to be." I loved the peace of that mosque, after the cacophony of the Old City. With Scheherezade, after a long and tiring walk, the two of us just chose to lie down in the front alcove, not exactly the place for women. But we needed the sweetness of the marble beneath us, the shade, and the fans, placed obviously to shield the devout from Lahore's blistering heat. Her husband, Zahoor—the avant-garde artist—was quite appalled to see his women lie where they should not be. "Please get up, please get up," he begged, while Scheherezade and I ignored him, happy to place our spines on marble's peace.

Was it peace that Mamma got from Pip? I doubt it. Consider for her the astonishment of traveling from London to Karachi, with her small babe (my darling) in her arms. In 1948 the British had left, yes, but what an ethnic reminder she must have been of a race that should have been gone! She behaved with tentative propriety to a necessarily suspicious culture, and when Pip set up the *Times of Karachi* with his partner, Amir Ali Fancy, I do believe she cheered. I thought of her when running through Yale corridors and a student politely stopped me. "I wanted to let you know, I am Tita Fancy," she said. My heart stopped with burdens of memory. "You are Amir Ali's daughter?" I asked. "His granddaughter," she replied. She was my student, as others have been, bringing back names into my life that wrench me, punctiliously, into the past.

I was thinking as much, in terms of ideas of order, when Austin and I viewed our Maine farm and I asked him to explain points that I, urban as I was, wished to know. "Where do the trout go in the winter?" I questioned. "I've no idea," he replied succinctly. "And who eats up the little chickabiddies?" "I don't know." So I learned to be more imaginative. When I watched him feed the upstairs sheep (yes, Pip, he is still my husband, you'll be glad to know), I thought what a wonderfully bucolic sight he must seem to a passerby, a shepherd positively, tending to his flock! Only I was close enough to hear him say, "Get out of my way, you fucking stupid bastards!" And, Pip, since I wrote my dissertation in and around Wordsworth, you would understand my newly suspicious proximity with nature. It is somewhat odd. I have to come to terms with some salient facts: the chickens eat the sheep food, the sheep eat the duck food, the ducks eat the fish food, the fish eat the water lily food, and the dog eats everything—anything—that comes her way. A farm, with the beautiful Maine coastline ahead. "O nature, nature," it makes me exclaim, "will you ever keep life right?"

"O nature," we girls exclaimed in Pakistan, when once again the city of Lahore had run out of Tampax. Taxed as a luxury item throughout the world—which strikes me as abominably unfair—we were always in wait for Tampax. If a friend or relative went to Europe, the last thing in the world we wanted were some duty-free cigarettes: we wanted a bag full of those lightweight and indispensable dispensabilities. At times, however, supplies would fail. And then, with its unique talent for plagiarism, Pakistan produced a product of its own: it was called Yumpax. The box replicated in fine detail the Tampax container, but added the somewhat ominous line: "Another Yum-Yum Product!" Well, Yum-Yum, you got the better of me. After a huge struggle—private, of course—with the cardboard vessel, a Yumpax could indeed sail up and moor itself in our groins. Would that not be enough? No. For the Yum had ideas of its own and would choose to spread like one of those Japanese toys that you place in water. I can distinctly recall sitting with my sisters in an evening garden, while Pip strode out to us, a triumphant article in his hand. "It's reached its climax!" he proclaimed boisterously, while the Yum-Yum product in one of us was quietly growing, like a cauliflower or an anenome.

A saddening thought. But you were, Pip, always exuberant about your editorials and your articles, even when you did them every day. Think of the time in Rawalpindi after you had been—for a very brief time—colonel in the army and director of the Intelligence Agency. I was glad to have you home again, instead of going through that hideous routine of getting you dressed, shining the brass in your epaulettes (I promise that brass is known as "pips"), and reminding you to take your cap. My mother quite agreed and added ruefully, "He *couldn't* like the uniform!" Still, when you returned to our home in Lalazar, sitting out in the garden to write your piece, I had no idea that you paid any attention to things other than your words. And yet you did. Think of the fact that Tillat and Irfani had new pets, rabbits with the names of Chookie and Pookie, in my siblings' great inventiveness.

Pip was at first in adamant objection to the rabbits. "Do you know how these things breed?" he shouted. "As much as you do" was my response. But it turned out that the rabbits were both males, and so we never had a bunch of baby rabbits hopping round the garden: a regret for me, who even then was obsessed with things small. Chookie and Pookie were, however, gay and perfectly content with their own rather obvious maneuvers. They became part of the Lalazar household, and how we admired their ingenuity when they took to hopping across the street to eat our neighbors' grass because it happened to be greener! But some young street lad took a sling and killed them both: I had not expected Pip to notice, but in fact he was heart-sorrowed. "Don't talk to me about it!" he muttered. "I would be sitting out here in the sun, writing about Muslim nationhood, and those bunnies would be jumping round me—more than you ever do!" He had much love inside him, in some extraneous fashion: I even believe he came to love Mars.

Mars was a Samoyed, and now I truly feel shamed at the lack of originality with which we named our pets, for his mate was named Venus. We loved those dogs, so it was hard to see our Venus trot out and mate with a *Kan Gulu*—hideous fighting dogs, with cropped ears and tails. Nonetheless, when Venus went out to bear his litter, she came back close to dead. And when they arrived, those minuscule *Kan Gulus*, how desperately she worked to give them life! They would not live to see her udder, no matter how hard she strove to make them realize their lives. Venus, exhausted, died a few hours afterward. People—for people always like to correct me—tell me that dogs do not have udders. Venus did, I say with some misery, because I watched her work desperately at her *Kan Gulus*, trying in vain to make those morsel bodies reach her tired tits.

Mars survived. Perhaps he was happier without her, no competition at all in terms of our affection. So through the wars, Marq, as the cooks called him, returned to us always with a doglike joy. I used to say, "Marqoo, out of the way," when he lay wagging on our front veranda. "Oh, Mars, get out of the way," I'd say on my return from the university. Mars would look up, give the promise of a wag, and then lie down. The day he died, Tillat swears to me, was the end of her childhood.

But then there were also cats. I wasn't particularly fond of those finicky animals, but we had them still. "Sara, how can you," Mamma would say when I brushed with some severity a kitten off my lap. But I simply did not like them. That can only be my fault. Think of Irfan, my baby brother, sobbing, as he carried in a dying kitten in his arms. It was Kaloo Mere Aloo (roughly translated "you black one, my potato": you see, it rhymed). I hated to think that youngsters could die and further hated it when Tillat's kitten, named by the second generation with far greater ingenuity White Paws Kiri Karo, was caught in the swinging kitchen door and almost lost his tail. "It's no matter," said the bearer soothingly. "It's no matter at all." "It *is* a matter," wailed Tillat and Irfan, and as a consequence Kiri Karo must have lived for centuries. Aside from his broken tail, which he bore as a token, something else broke his tongue, which dangled from his mouth most indelicately and made him unable to clean, as cats do, their obviously cleanable fur. Instead, he mouthed silent noises at us, ghoulishly celebrating his own infirmities. But I disliked poor Kiri Karo, particularly when he jumped into my lap with friendliness and sent the cloud of dust around him at me. My expression must have been the same as when Ifat's little baby, Ayesha, always chose to urinate on my lap, cascading through nappies and all. I suppose it could be considered a gesture of welcome or affection.

And my Irfan, why did he have such an inordinate need for pets? There was his snake, his doves, his little baby quail. The latter was in Islamabad. "I'm going to call him my pecker," he told Ifat, proudly. Ifat, not knowing how to enlighten him, simply beamed back, "Aha." What a summer it was. I arrived late, because that was the year a DC-10 had lost its wing somewhere, and all similar machines had to be grounded. We were in Amsterdam for a while, then we took off, only to be told several hours later into the night, "Ladies and gentlemen, welcome to— Amsterdam." Apparently an authority had insisted that we backtrack. As some thought of conciliation, they took us on a barge tour the following morning. Consider the sight: a group of extremely gaunt and disoriented travelers, hoping to see Pakistan, and seeing instead the waterways of— Amsterdam.

But after the quail was eaten by an eagle, I think, Irfan continued to add color to the summer by showing off in front of Ifat's children, slipping and breaking his thumb. Ifat and I were at our most efficient. Ignoring Pip's bellow, "What's happening?"—we bundled him into the car and raced off that summer evening, first to a nearby doctor and then to the hospital. The doctor's house was daunting, guarded as it was by a most ferocious dog. "No, Ifat, we can't afford to be bitten by a mad dog at this moment," I said. It reminded me of the time in Lahore, some years earlier, when Tillat and I were perambulating across the fields from our house to Ifat's. There we came across a dead mongoose, not a pleasant sight. "You know what a dead mongoose means, Tillat," I hissed. "Live snake! Run!" And without further discussion on the matter, we ran. Consider the time of Mamma's funeral, with everyone sleeping in exhausted disarray, when Irfan told Nuz the following morning, "Nuz! You slept in my bed with my snake!" Nuz was quite appalled, assuming him to be troubled and figurative, until Irfan pulled back his pillow, and there it was—green and comfortable—his snake.

I think each of us died in some way the day they buried Mamma. There was a special providence about her, and part of me wishes I could have seen her face when I dedicated my dissertation to her and to you, Pip, with that uncanny Wordsworthian phrase "Was it for this?" Nuz was troubled by that phrase at first. I explicated; she understood; henceforth you could see her muttering—when a car refused to start or an egg refused to boil—"Was it for this?" She loved Mamma with a peculiar intensity: not that she did not love you too, Pip, and all of us, but it is strange to contemplate the devotion she conferred, unerringly, upon her stepmother.

I am not even sure how Mamma would have responded to *Meatless Days*, although of course she couldn't, since it is largely an elegy for her. But I cannot describe my trepidation when I sent the book to Pip. I annotated it with little justifications and clarifications, or, when my ingenuity failed me, "Please don't read this para, Pip!" my note would beg. Para—a paragraph—is that an entirely subcontinental expression?

Perhaps it is, because occasionally my students do look at me strangely when I say, "You've got to put more punch into this para!" I was scared that my father would assume I was making fun of him, whereas I was only loving him, a difficult thing to explain. On the whole, he took it quite well, although he expressed some disgust at my inability to martial facts as exactly as he did. Pip certainly was a great martialer of facts, and he took exception when my more literary bent took liberties with his beloved history, the history of Pakistan. But then he looked at me memorably—his lion's head always had a memorable gaze—and said to me, "On Judgment Day, I will say to God, 'Be merciful, for I have already been judged by my child.'" Months later in New Haven, a colleague of mine was asking interestedly about my family's reaction to the work, and I repeated Pip's sentence to him. David looked up with undiluted admiration. "That's the best line in the book," he said.

Upright in politics?—completely. But not quite so upright with his children. Given our knowledge of Pip's penchant for reading, today I cannot understand why my siblings and I would faithfully keep diaries and secret letters that Pip would equally faithfully find and read. Was it our sexual exploits he was looking for? It can't be, because we really didn't have that many. But I was reminded of his old habit in comparatively recent times when mad Tom wrote me an amorous letter in his extravagant fashion. It missed me, but it certainly did not miss Pip. The next time we spoke, he muttered, "You had a letter from some Tom." "And how do you know?" I asked politely. "I read it." And before I could begin to expostulate on privacy and other fine points, he added: "It was porno." "Well, then, I hope you enjoyed it!" I exclaimed with indignation, but Pip was completely unabashed. "It was porno," he kept repeating. Now in heaven, Pip, you must put these things from your mind. You see me married, domesticated. But one thing I know still agitates you. Sometimes in the middle of the night, I can hear you whisper, "Make him a Muslim; make Austin a Muslim!" The last time we met, Pip, you repeated your plea, adding, "You know, if you convert someone to Islam, you go straight to heaven!" He didn't add, but it was in his eyes, "This is your one chance of getting there, Sara, so why not give it a try?"

My husband would be quite astounded at such a proposition, and not being the best of Mozzies myself, I do not intend to try. His forays into the *desi,* the Paki worlds, are still tentative, although it is my bitter regret that the two of you never met, Pip. You would have got such pleasure if you had been present at our recent trip to Chicago and watched Austin have his first-ever conversation with a drag queen. He was a guest of our hosts, a *desi* poet, making a flamboyant entry. "Darling," he said to me, "move over: you may be the princess but I'm the queen, and I want a piece of him, too!" Austin was transfixed. The poet called him honey, Goody Goody Yearie Yearie, and in general made himself endearing. Later, when we had a minute to ourselves, Austin asked me quite earnestly, "What is the religious sect in India that requires men to wear jewelry, silks, and lipstick?" "I'll explain later," I replied.

I was there to give a reading from this selfsame text, and I cannot tell you how gratified I was when Memon Sahib and C. M. Naim Sahib told me that mine was a perfect title. I responded to those distinguished Urdu scholars that the title was in fact my father's: he would frequently announce that he was going to write his autobiography and call it *Boys Will Be Boys,* and then would burst into a roar of laughter. And Naim told us an anecdote of how at some crucial Muslim League conference in Delhi, Jinnah got up and announced, "All right, boys. And now get to work for Pakistan!" I was touched by that tale: how appropriate it felt, for whose boy were you, Pip, other than that of the man you would call—time after repeated time—"My Leader"? And are you still, uncouth swain, bellowing out or whispering to yourself, "My Leader"?

زندگانی کی حقیقت کوہکن کے دِل سے پوچھ!
اقبال

Ask of Kohakan's heart the reality of existence!

— I Q B Ā L

*I*t was in my father's wake that Eqbal Ahmad said to me over the phone, "What a man he was, Z.A., what a man!" I was a trifle surprised at his appreciation, because there could hardly be two more different readers of politics. "You know, Sara, when I read *My Leader*—and I came from a Congress family—I nearly was converted." I listened. "Nearly, but not quite," he added charmingly. It still makes my mind boggle to think of Jinnah, that fastidious, that secular man, becoming the champion— of all things—for Muslim nationhood. Was he more interested in the political reality of minorities than he was in religion? It had to be the case. I don't believe he truly spoke Urdu, and I cannot remember on how many countless Independence Days, Pakistan Resolution Days, we had to listen to the radio rebroadcasting one of his final speeches. "Now what we must do, my fellow citizens," Jinnah pronounced in his clipped English, "is work, work, work." Twice yearly Pip would listen to that injunction and repeat, with awe and such affection, "Work, work, work."

And certainly he did work, work, work, even before Independence and the subsequent death of Jinnah. *My Leader* was an accomplishment: it elicited a letter of thanks from Jinnah, who declared it was a great honor "for a man like you to express such warm appreciation for the services I may have rendered to the Muslim nation." That sentence won Pip's heart. How many times he had said to his assembled family: "'*May* have rendered, *may* have rendered'! What self-deprecation, what modesty!" I have my doubts, because I don't think Jinnah was a particularly modest man. But to Pip, he was impeccable. After the sad sundering of India—I still believe that it was sad—who was there to sustain the fervor of the Muslim League? It is still hard to believe that now there have been at least three generations, and at least as many wars, since India was, even putatively, one. I regret that Mīrzā Ghālib's tomb is in so-called "enemy country" and that Kashmir, more beautiful than it is fabled to be, should become such a hideous travesty of its inherent peace and—more pointedly—its waterways. We will not even mention Bangladesh at this point, with its soul-destroying loss of lives.

Let us turn instead to the year that I knew I had to leave, to a tale that I will doubtless return to again. When, in 1976, I finally convinced Pip, "Papa, I simply have to leave," that sentence wrought confusion to our family in Lahore. He was told the truth, but not the whole truth, so all of us had to work quite hard to keep our stories straight. "Don't ask me these questions, Zia," said Mamma in her inimitable fashion. "I always get the answers wrong." But, nonetheless, the day of my departure arrived, and what did Pip do? He handed me a copy of the Quran. I looked at him, keeping a completely straight face, and I read its rather touching inscription. "For my darling daughter Sara," he wrote. "Even if I had the whole Creation at my disposal to choose a present from, I could not choose a more precious one than this Divine Message which reveals the true significance of life. I commend it to you for study and reflection in order to gain an insight into the very meaning of knowledge in whose quest you are undertaking this journey to the United States. Papa." "Honestly, Tillat," I grumbled to my sister, "I have to leave all my books behind and yet I have to lug along a Quran?" I very nearly didn't. For some explicable or inexplicable reason, I forgot to pack it, although I was sure not to forget the little wooden ashtray that my Irfan had crafted for me. "The Quran!" said Pip at the airport. "The Quran!" So my poor brother was sent back home posthaste to collect my absent gift, which was delivered to me seconds before my flight left from Lahore. "A good omen," said my father solemnly. And so I had to arrive in America, as good Mozzies should, with a Quran tucked under my arm.

I still have it, Pip. Not that I have ever been compelled to read its wisdom or the appended commentary by the sagacious translator Marmaduke Pickthall. For that name alone he deserved to be a Muslim. I must keep it for your tidy writing—usually so untidy—and for the fact that your heart lurched for me to reenter Islam. Remember that I was not really there for long. I was not born in London, as two of your other children were, but we were transplanted soon enough to think of London as our home, such as homes be. And you were so secular then, with politics and nationhood swarming from your discourse into our brains. Islam notwithstanding, your handwriting still can wrench me, as your Quran has traveled with me—and will travel—from home to home.

Pip was touched himself, when I took back to Lahore a letter I had recently received from the son of Pothan Joseph. He, as a former editor of *Dawn*, had written to me a gently chiding letter. *Dawn* was not founded in Karachi, as apparently I had claimed, but somewhere else, when my father was his father's subeditor. Mr. Joseph proceeded to describe Pip's quirks and intensities, all too well known to me. He concluded this letter from Bombay by writing, charmingly, "Please excuse my puckish manner," and had the sweetness of soul to seek out and send to me pictures of Pip when he first worked at *Dawn*. When I looked at the photographs of that young man—with a face disturbingly like my own—I knew that if I did not love him already, I would until God's heavenly Muslim universe had descended and taken him from me for good.

What a strange contour map we could create by simply making a geography of all the places of our births! My parents, of course, born continents apart, but then their children: I do not even remember where Nuz, Baji's daughter, was born—perhaps Simla—but then there was Ifat in London, Shahid and me in Karachi, Tillat in Lahore, and Irfan in London again. Amidst so much movement, it makes me wonder what happened to our filaments of identity, whether they bruised, strengthened, or simply became themselves. But much of them must remain necessarily rooted in Lahore—"Oh, City of Lights," the poet Faiz called it—the grave-homes of our mother, our sister, and now our father.

There is an archaeology to Lahore: the Mall itself, one of its central and delicate arteries, lined with stately trees and public gardens; the beautiful grounds of Aitchison College, school temporarily of both my brothers; and Lawrence Gardens, which post-partition Lahore solemnly renamed Bagh-e-Jinnah, but in my day that name certainly didn't work. Even the most Lahori of taxi- and rickshaw drivers obstinately insisted on its prior name: "Bagh-e-Jinnah?" they would say, dubiously. "Oh! Lahrance Garrden!" And I think they would feel similarly about the now officially nameless Charing Cross, the pleasant swatch of green that lies after the Governor's House and sits beyond the elegant building of the General Assembly. Given its elegance, I simply wish that an aesthetic if not political desire would make the assembly convene more frequently. It didn't.

Nonetheless, that little patch of green of Charing Cross saw some remarkable striations, good news for any archaeologist. There was a sweet pavilion at its center, a little marble edifice that housed in my childhood a larger-than-life statue of Queen Victoria, herself much in bronze. She was represented as sitting (did she ever do anything but sit?), but that familiar posture of repose was soon to leave our lives. One morning I noticed that Victoria had somehow unceremoniously left the pavilion. In her place was an aquarium, a fish show for the public's delight. I could not quite see the logic. But I did see the inexorability when, on one of my last trips to Pakistan, the aquarium had vanished. In its place, in the

Charing Cross pavilion, a huge cement *rehal* had been placed. I'll explain
that. Suffice it to say that it purported to be a Holy Book Stand for an
invisible Quran, almost as large as Victoria.

No one knew where Victoria vanished to, with all her cumbersome
bronze. I do not think that I have ever seen her reappear in the Lahore
Museum, although much work must have been lavished on producing
that incongruity, but where did she go? Not, I believe, to the museum,
although that would have been her most appropriate house. Maybe even
bronze can be recycled, or thrown away, so that no official would have
to deal with memory. Metal can be soft. Like a historical tale, metal can
be a permeable medium, letting in sentences where sentences should
not be bred. Too many germs are attracted to history and are prone to
riot in its curfewed streets. No wonder Lahore pretends at hygiene, even
as it becomes one of the most polluted of polluted cities. After Victoria,
however, why preserve Kipling? Kim's Gun with the supreme air of a
nonviolent object sat before the museum and the university, accruing
daily affection. The aplomb of that icon can rarely be replicated in my
life, when on my daily trip to the university, "Oh, Kipling, Kipling," it
would move me to utter.

For, most incongruously, it is hard for my life to move away from
Kipling. Aside from his gun and the *Civil and Military Gazette* of Lahore, there is the most peculiar fact that he continued to pop up, geo-
graphically speaking, in most unexpected circumstances. There was Rottingdean next to Brighton, the village where my uncle Hugh lived: down
the road from him was the Kipling House, which Hugh's family considered buying, until the village turned it into the Kipling House Museum.
Good for Rottingdean. Yet I was slightly perplexed when I was invited
to give a talk at the Kipling House in Vermont with my friend and colleague Murray, and we did it, bringing Austin along with us. But then to
be given the honor of sleeping in Kipling's bedroom, pristinely maintained, was not a joy I had anticipated. Did Austin and I honestly have
to curve ourselves up and sleep in the very bed of the man who wrote,
"Oh, East is East, and West is West, and never the twain shall meet"? But
we did. Strangely enough, there was a Lama kind of brass bowl next to
the bed, which I profanely filled with cigarette butts.

I think you would have enjoyed the evening in Vermont, Pip, because you liked to hear me speak of Lahore, and you were also fond of Kipling. Do you remember when the Lama squats next to a letter writer to dictate a missive to the Fathers telling them that he would buy an education for Kim? There was an old man—straight out of Kipling—who would sit on a stool outside the Gulberg Post Office in Lahore, beneath a tattered umbrella. There people would come to dictate their letters, beneath a sign that read: "Latter Writer." I often wondered what that old man's dreams must have been like, after having spent the entire day transcribing—for a very paltry sum—other people's longings. A letter from a wife to a bondsman husband in Kuwait; from a son in the city to his village family; from a man to his former employer, hopelessly asking for restitution. Kipling would have divined many tales from those sights, for he loved Lahore, although he would also call it with its scorching summer—most accurately—"City of the Dreadful Night." From City of Lights to City of the Dreadful Night: we have come full circle.

كوئی ویرانی سی ویرانی ہے
غالب

There is a wilderness within the wilderness

— GHĀLIB

*H*ow furniture travels. I can still recall how strange it felt when we returned to Pakistan after our sojourn in London to see again those beautiful old bookcases, the sideboards, and numerous other wooden objects
that had been stored in our dear uncle Shamim's safekeeping in Karachi.
I had forgotten them, but there was something even in the grain of that
wood that told me, "We are yours; you are ours." We could have been
moles, all of us, from *The Wind in the Willows*, acknowledging that, yes,
objects possess a certain dignified patience and that they have a life that
waits for one's return. Mole forgot his home when he took up with Ratty
and the life of the River, but it called him back, imperiously, when he

walked into its ambit. That's how I felt when I encountered the furniture of my infancy: "We have a better memory than you do," the bookshelves told me. "We have attended your return."

For some reason, the only objects that my parents took with them to London were their Persian carpets—hardly easy items to ship, but I think Mamma could not live without their intricate patterns of existence. I remember her laughing, when she was in charge of selling our London home preparatory to our return to Pakistan, that all potential buyers who stopped by were far more taken with the carpets than the house. Today, it strikes me as extremely unfair that she had to do all that alone— you had taken yourself back, Pip, to head the *Pakistan Times* in Lahore— but she did. And then she had to pack, and cope with the movers, and contemplate the most significant object of all: the peripatetic piano.

The piano. It belonged to my grandfather in Wales and, after his death, was shipped with some difficulty to us in London. It was an arresting, charming mahogany upright, and before his stroke, Grandpa—who sang professionally in his spare time from his insurance business—used to play and sing for us whenever we visited Wales. He had a lovely baritone voice that I think my brother Shahid inherited from him, although these days I wish Shahid would sing rather than shout and conduct his life a few decibels lower. So the piano came to London, where Mamma would play and we would sing around her: there was a sweetness to that family ritual that belies ordinary description. But what must that Brinsmead piano have thought, when out of the blue it was crated up and shipped off to Pakistan? Was it playing "Men of Harlech" inside itself or "God Bless the Prince of Wales"?

Nonetheless, those cartons were shipped off to Lahore and must have sat far too long at a Karachi dock, because when they reached our home in Model Town, their contents were close to ruined. I recall how my mother's hands shook when the workmen opened those evil wooden boxes and she made—for insurance purposes, I suppose—an inventory of items and the damage they had sustained. "One Isphanani carpet," she wrote down, "rotted to sod." "One Brinsmead piano corroded with sea salt." Once again, she was doing this alone: was the *Pakistan Times* so important, Pip, that you couldn't have taken a day off and have been there to comfort her trembling hands? We children tried, but we were not enough. We heard the sickening sound of the wooden boxes being torn apart; we saw my grandfather's uprooted piano being wheeled away, its mahogany floating in the air like sad ribbons.

I am glad to say we got it back. After a laborious search, we found a piano tuner in Lahore who also repaired pianos. His name was Mr. Pearl and he was a dainty, methodical little man who came every day for several weeks until the piano began to look and sound like itself. When Mr. Pearl finished the job, he politely handed his final bill to my father, almost curtsied, and then was gone. "He is a pearl of great price," said my father, and then roared with laughter, as he always did at his own jokes. But at least the piano was upright again, and in the evening—to the astonishment of our neighbors listening to Ravi Shankar—the air would be rent with Mamma's children singing lustily:

"Men of Harlech, are ye waking?
Saxon hosts your hills are shaking!"

The piano went with us to Rawalpindi and then back to Lahore again; it almost was shipped to Kuwait but didn't quite make it. After Mamma died and our home was being dismantled, Tillat was to have the piano. She was the only one of us—with extraordinary skill—who taught herself how to play. So Tillat was to take Grandpa's piano to Kuwait, but I'm glad she didn't, for what would the Iraqi soldiers invading her home have done to it? Kicked it? "I didn't mind those soldiers coming in and taking what they considered valuable," Tillat later said to me. "But the thought that strangers were in my house, looking at my books and photographs, was truly killing to me." So the piano sat in neglected storage in Lahore, until my sister's last trip there, when she hit upon a brilliant idea. She called up her former school, the Convent of Jesus and Mary, and asked the nuns if they could use another piano. The nuns were ecstatic. So now that cosmopolitan musical instrument is installed for the rest of its life in a convent, in Lahore. Beside it is a little brass plaque, probably quite puzzling to an outsider, for it reads: "In loving memory of Surraya Mair Suleri, daughter of John Amos Jones."

It gave me a pang at first, which is very stupid, for what else could have been done? Ship it to me at a royal price to Brooklin, Maine, or New Haven, Connecticut? Or to Shahid in Provence? Or have Tillat heft it along with her as she moved to Vancouver, Canada? No, the instrument has grown roots of its own and now is as much at home in Lahore as is Kim's Gun. Grandpa would have been happy to know it was in use, that little girls in their white crisp uniforms were banging at it every day. I wonder what they could be playing and which ghosts emanate as they touch the keys.

Mamma would also have been pleased, for she disliked to see an object vacant of its use in the world, as far as objects go. This certainly was not true of her relations with people. As far as people went, Mamma was a veritable pied piper, moving quietly along with a string of lame ducks in her wake. "Oh, Mamma, not another one," we'd groan, when we returned to see a chirpy lame duck long overstaying his welcome and talking incessantly over his tea. "You see," she would say apologetically after the duck's departure, "he is my student whose father has died . . ." "Everyone's father dies," I responded lucidly. "Does that mean we have to have the world for tea?" "Sara!" she'd say. "For shame!" and then would go on to do exactly as she pleased. Pip would call this motley collection "Mamma's pigeons," perhaps with Trafalgar Square in mind. Mamma met our objections with a little smile and would continue to tell us stories as preposterous as Pip's, although in a lower key. A student at the university had come into her office with a string of anxious questions about an exam or a paper, which Mamma answered generously, adding—in her kind fashion—"Let me know if there is any other way in which I can help you." "Oh, yes, Mrs. Suleri," replied the young woman eagerly. "You can! Please advise me about my skin!" "Your *skin*?" "Yes, Mrs. Suleri, I have such bad acne, I don't know what to do!" Mamma gave her as much dermatological advice as she could muster at such short notice, and then smiled to indicate that the interview was over. Instead, the girl leapt up, exclaiming, "Oh, Mrs. Suleri, please let me kiss you!" A startled Mamma still politely proffered the girl her cheek.

That's what we mean about lame ducks. If she was ready to proffer cheeks to acne faces in her office, of what other incongruity was she not capable? I certainly cannot claim to be as undisciplined myself. At Yale I had a student of Japanese extraction who came to my office to complain bitterly that despite all her interest in the theater, she had only been asked to audition for *South Pacific*. I was consoling, and not too surprised when she later wrote a one-woman play for herself to act in, titled *The Yellow Lady Sings the Blues*. Despite my best intentions, I could not will myself to sit through that performance. The student seemed unperturbed, and when she came to say good-bye at the end of the semester, she asked me, "Professor Suleri, may I embrace you?" For a second, my office seemed petrifyingly full of ducks. I leaned back in my chair and answered with a friendly sagacity, "I think not." It seemed to be a satisfactory resolution, but when I repeated the incident to Pip, he was surprisingly appalled. "Sara! How could you be so cruel?" he reproached. Nettled, I replied, "Well, Pip, what would *you* do if a *chaprasi* or a *chowkidar* walked into your office and said, 'Suleri Sahib, let me give you a hug'?" Pip did not respond, but our joint silence seemed to confirm what an extremely unlikely eventuality my analogy had been.

Pip would still go to the UN in those days, for the General Assembly, so it was simple for me to catch a train in New Haven and nip down to New York to see him. And so we met in overfurnished hotel rooms, although we did not stay in the same hotel, for reasons that I will explain anon. He was relatively at home in New York, but I could tell that he preferred London, even as he was blisteringly funny about the tedium of the UN. "How did Mamma do it?" he mused to me at the Oak Room, a bar he loved. He had been descanting about the boredom of that day's session and was happy to sit back and muse about Mamma's pigeons. "They must have been so boring, pigeon after pigeon." "And duck after duck," I added. We thought about how unlikely her imagination had been, and how patient, until it was time to leave that furniture aside and turn to other things.

A year or so later, in the aftermath of the Gulf War, I spent the summer in London, staying with Tillat in her furnished house. As I have mentioned, we were quite a crowd, with Tillat and her children, a convalescent Pip, me, and Shahid around from morn till night. Shahid had been very good at arranging for Pip's eye operation—with a specialist from

Harley Street, to Pip's great satisfaction, for he believed in names—but in his convalescence, Shahid could not resist teasing him. While still in the hospital, Pip was asked what he wanted for lunch. He turned aside and muttered, "Sausages." Pork is prohibited to Mozzies. "*Pork* sausages?" queried Shahid. "No. Meat sausages," Pip replied gruffly. "But what *kind* of meat? Ah, I understand! *That* meat!" And then Shahid began to sing with great gusto, "Give me a bash / of bangers and mash / my mother used to make!" Before lunch arrived, however, the nurse announced that Pip had some religious-looking visitors coming up. Pip, aghast, turned to Shahid: "Get rid of the sausages! Hide the sausages!" he hissed frantically, while Shahid just gazed at him, with a fond paternal smile.

Later, at Tillat's, where Shahid and I had created a cozy little room in her garage, Pip would come and join us, ostensibly for a cigar. We welcomed him; he sat down and then glanced at the glasses in our hands. After a while he announced, "I think I am thirsty." "How stupid of me, Pip!" exclaimed Shahid, leaping up. "What would you like? Mango juice? Coca-Cola? Yogurt and water?" Pip turned away and muttered, "Scorch." "What?" said Shahid, feigning deafness. "Scorch," Pip repeated into his shoulder. "Oh!" said Shahid. "Scotch!" And then as loud as he could: "SCOTCH AND SODA!" As Shahid happily prepared the drink, Pip looked around furtively, as though Tillat's neighbors were at least as vigilant as the Ayatollah Khomeini.

Silly tales. But sometimes my mind feels quite unfurnished, Pip, even when I live in this quaintly historical home in Maine, with objects like our bookshelves all around us. I will not be sentimental enough to do a Yeats (which I often do) and say, "I must lie down where all the ladders start, / In the foul rag-and-bone shop of the heart." No, instead my memory is concentrated. It sees you keenly, Pip, waiting for one of us to emerge and hitting on the piano keys—you were a most impatient man—a one-two-three, one-two-three, on Grandpa's piano in the hallway. Did that aged ivory give you any inkling of how overfurnished and cluttered with ideas you may be? I have no choice; my ladder's gone and I shall reiterate, "I must lie down where all the ladders start, / In the foul rag-and-bone shop of the heart."

میرا سونا شہر، قصوری!

My golden town, Kasur!

— BABY NUR JEHAN, POPULAR SONG

It was during the 1971 war, when I was staying with Ifat in Rawalpindi, that I first registered the existence of the border town Kasur, subsequently to play a somewhat daunting role in our existence. Ifat's husband was off fighting in Bengal, in a war I do not wish to dwell upon, and we were numbed, frozen, listening to the radio play night and day, in Ifat's in-laws' house, the Brigardier's pink house on the hill. In the midst of dreary blackouts, we heard the radio give us news that was not believable, and then blast out song after song of patriotic music. I softened toward the Brigardier when he barked out, "Gadzooks! 'My beloved and beautiful town, Kasur'? That little backwater? Why not sing, 'My beloved and beautiful town, Gujranwala'?" They didn't, and the Queen of Melody, Baby/Bebe Nur Jehan, kept pelting out her songs at us, "Oh, my golden town, Kasur-ni, my golden town, Kasur-ni." There was white terror on my sister's face, but when we thought about "Oh, my beloved and beautiful town, Gujranwala," we had to laugh. It didn't even scan.

But I must tell the truth. At this point, I do not wish to hold forth with an Ifat story, although so many are in my mind. And I will certainly not speak of Tillat as easily as I did, since she cut me to the quick by saying, quite recently, "Sara, you do not know how to keep a confidence." Not true. If I speak to people I trust, Moon-face, that should not trouble you. So let us tread the weary road together, from Lahore unto Kasur.

My stepsister, Shahida, needs to be represented in low colors, hues dim, and even then an average intelligence would surmise that I exaggerate. Pip has to be given some credit for his ingenuity. While at the *Pakistan Times* after Mamma's and Ifat's deaths, and after I would not return, he was indeed bereft of a companion. What could you do, Pip, when a lady from the advertising department came up to declare that her superior was harassing her sexually? As editor of the newspaper, Pip fired him forthwith—although in retrospect, even you, Pip, would agree that the poor man was probably quite innocent. In any case, you became a champion for that beleaguered woman, and the next thing that we knew, we had a stepsister, hailing from no other place but Kasur. "*You* are now my father," she told Pip, energetically. "There is no one here for me but you!"

I am conscious of the fact that I have been delaying this subject, the entry of Shahida into our lives. I feel slightly on tiptoe, even as I contemplate the phenomenon that is Shahida. Now you know, readers, why I didn't stay at the Plaza with Pip: he said with false heartiness, "You two sisters can share a room together!" My heart began to fail. I had already endured the astonishment of walking down Fifth Avenue with this unknown lady, and her seizing my hand and swinging it, chanting, "Gold-nail-polish, gold-nail-polish!" That was the object of her search. My father looked on indulgently at such girlish antics, at which point I honestly believe I could have killed him. I was more than silenced and caught the 1:00 A.M. Metro-North back to New Haven.

Let it be known, I am quite fond of Shahida. She adopted my father, not he, her. And there she was, a phenomenon. In a twinkling of an eye, she had moved in, and the furniture we children loved was banished to the *radi wallah,* the rag-and-bone man, for perhaps a reasonable profit. And so when we returned, it was as though Martha Stewart had visited with her cultural vacuum cleaner: there was nothing we recognized, nothing, except heart-searing stuff such as my mother's beloved china being converted into corn and flour scoops. When I got the courage to query "Why?" while I visited Lahore, Shahida looked at me as though I were an imbecile. "Too old–too old–too old," she said, and had banished whatever remained to Kasur. And so when the rest of us came to our father's house in Lahore, it was to be confronted with a Kasur architecture—there were shiny curtains on each window, an unusually novel dining table, and Pip's *gatha* gone for good. The *gatha* needs explication: it was a piece of hardboard that the workers in one of our several moves had left lying around. Pip looked at it and decided it would be a perfect implement for him to rest his work upon, and then used it daily, so who knows how many governments had their fall or confirmation upon Pip's *gatha.* But Shahida threw it away. She also reupholstered Pip's favorite armchair, so that its faded green became a brocade quite shocking to the eye. Let me repeat, I am fond of Shahida.

There are certain moments, however, that deserve recording. For one thing, I could not quite comprehend Shahida's obsession with figurines. In every room and everywhere you looked, there was a figurine to arrest your attention: a laughing gnome upon a toadstool, a coyly amorous French shepherd and shepherdess, a languorous lover with a nightingale. Where on earth did she find them in Lahore, we asked. Ceramics there are galore, but beautiful blues, lovely earthen colors. And not a paint and gloss that coats a French shepherd, who looks up winking at you. The last time I returned, Shahida's formidable cascade of hair had turned positively blond: I tried a polite compliment on her change of ways, at which point she responded, with a pout she has perfected, "Oh, no, this is natural." There was always a shine to Shahida.

And then the phrases she has added to our vocabulary! One of our favorites is "thinning-just-like-Sara's." And it was not my torso that was the point of reference: not at all, it was my hair. "In the beginning," said Shahida with a kind beam toward me, "my hair was-thinning-just-like-Sara's. But then, since I have started taking Feefol, the iron supplement, look what has happened!" In evidence, she tossed her forest of a mane at us. Since then, my siblings have adopted that phrase, so that in order to refer to my or anyone's iniquities, they add: "thinning-just-like-Sara's." Furthermore, I do not know how Tillat and I could do without the epithet "choosy." (Since this has been an oral tradition, Tat, how should we spell it? "choosy" or "choosie"?) We were sitting in an Islamabad bedroom, listening to Shahida hold forth; I held my calm as she told us about the Chinese restaurant that she and Pip liked to frequent, in order to eat "chicken-chong-mong." Calm was wearing thin, however, when she with an eagerness and intense rapidity of speech turned to describe a college friend to us. Why did we need this information, I wondered. "And-she-would-fuss-so-much-and-have-so-many-qualms-about-everything-we-decided-to-call-her-*Choosy!-Choosy!*" One of my fatal flaws is an uncontrollable laugh—call it an inelegant guffaw, if you will—and once it exploded from me, I had to leave the room. Nevertheless, the word remained to take its home among us. It is really quite beautiful, with a suppleness few other words possess. "I am feeling choosy, Sara," Tillat would say when she was homesick. "Tillat, I was so angry that I became quite choosy," I'd say, recounting some university imbecility. As a word it is quite lovely, and I do not believe we could do without its magnificent permutations. And you, Pip, choosy boy, where were you when such crucial exchanges transpired?

Somewhere else, perhaps embarrassed by your new daughter. It made you a trifle unwelcoming—most uncharacteristic of you—for when Nuz flew from Karachi to join us in Islamabad, you were peculiarly subdued. What a trip that was. Nuz had a rocky flight, and her temperament was not one to take such things lightly. Once home, before anything else, she took off her sari blouse, put it on her head, and knelt down to say some prayers of thanks to the God who had allowed her to arrive safely. "But, Nuz," I wondered, "does God really like to see you in a bra?" Maybe he did, for she was quite inviting. Mozzies, you see, must cover their heads when they pray, and Nuz simply grabbed the garment closest to her—her sari blouse. I am glad to say that I have photographs of that extraordinary act of devotion.

But what a summer that was. There was an Eid festival, and in order to be celebratory, we women actually mixed some *mehndi*, some henna, with which to decorate our palms and—if we were patient—the soles of our feet. Tillat was meticulous, making Mughal-like curlicues of great intricacy, but I insisted on the right to do one of Nuzzi's palms. "I'll put on it something that completely expresses your psyche!" I told her. She was quite content to lie back and hand me her palm, but less content when she washed her hand and saw that I had inscribed a bold "YES/NO" upon it. Henna takes at least a month before its vivid orange fades, so Nuz knew she would be flashing "YES/NO" to a perplexed audience for some weeks to come when she returned to Karachi.

It was during that vacation and reunion that we were able to observe Heba, such a baby chatterbox, make Pip's face soften as somehow his daughters could no longer do. And her mother, Tillat, felt sure that after the blistering sand of Kuwait, her daughter Heba would love to run barefoot, with her brother, on the monsoon-dampened grass of Islamabad. They did not. One evening I ran out in response to Heba's wail. She was standing in the garden flower beds, with rich alluvial soil oozing around her feet. "What's wrong, Heba?" I cried out as I ran to rescue her. She, a two-year-old, staring down at the mud surrounding her ankles, answered me with the aplomb of the greatest tragedian, "My toes!" Pip, you also liked the fact that sometimes her vocabulary would forsake her. Like me (I like to believe we are alike), she learned to speak very early. When idiom failed her, however, she would resort to a transfixing language. "Like that," she would say, "like that." Pip, you looked up at Heba's bitter sobbing, as you probably would not at ours. Heba ran into the dining room, slapped the table, and crying with indignation said, "Omi"—her brother, and with another smack upon the table—"like that, like that, like that."

For some reason, Shahida did not take very kindly to the children, except when she thought one of us was watching her. But she did, however, with great generosity, take charge of my wardrobe. On my summer trips I always wanted to stock up on Paki clothes but never had the strength to go to the market, buy the fabric, find a tailor, and tell the tailor master what design had been preoccupying my intelligence. During Ifat's life she would simply arrive with a pile of clothes to hand over to me, but that wondrous source had died. And so Shahida took over. She marched to Gulberg Market in Lahore, thinning-just-like-Sara, and bought for me a bunch of Lina Marias. That was the name of the designer, and it does perplex me to consider that a lady in Lahore could have been blessed with the name Lina Maria. The clothes were, ostensibly, *Shalimar-kameez*es. (I owe a debt of gratitude to Austin for that phrase: early in our acquaintance he asked me what my Paki clothes were called. "*Shalwar-kameez,*" I told him. "Oh! *Shalimar-kameez!*" he responded, and *Shalimar* it has been ever since.) Miss Lina Maria of Lahore had quite a remarkable concept of what a *Shalimar-kameez* should be. First, it should shine and slip, spurning cotton for the greater slither of polyester. It should ice itself with adornments where no adornments are really necessary. It could cunningly place a nipple—of fabric, of course— where a belly button would be far more appropriate. There was always a shine to Shahida.

No-dort—I am trying to quote her; and "no doubt" was always "no-dort"—I wore them, and even today Tillat will say to me, "I'm bringing you some Lina Marias, Sara. No—they're not Lina Marias; they are much nicer." No-dort they will be, but can you imagine, Tillat, what my feelings were when the summer after my marriage, Pip sent me off with Shahida to buy me a *desi* wedding gown? "But, Pip, I'm already married!" I protested, and he just smiled indulgently. So then, on a very hot summer afternoon, Shahida grabbed me by the arm and dragged me through the Old City of Lahore, bargaining vociferously with all the wedding-clothes vendors. If there is such a thing as a Ph.D. in haggling, she must have it, along with her other double M.A.'s. "No, no!" she told one vendor. "It has to be a silk *kurta*, because you see my sister"— glancing shyly down at her ample bosom—"my sister is not built like me." Her sister just stood there in a perspiration of chagrin and amazement: thinning-just-like-Sara. And to my surprise, I found myself chanting, as if for solace, "Lina Maria, Lina Maria, Lina Maria."

The garment itself is pretty—I am not denying that it is pretty—and must have added a good fifteen pounds to my sparse luggage, what with its heavily embroidered *dupatta*, its veil. And, in fact, I lugged it to London some years later, to wear for Shahid and Jane's wedding. I was glad to see them married, after all those years, and Irfan and I actually composed a song of praise for them. There is a remarkable Urdu film song that boasts of the refrain, "Three cheers for Bhabi, hip-hip-hooray, HIP-HIP-HOORAY!" Since *bhabi* means sister-in-law, Irfan and I thought it was a most appropriate tune. I wish I could remember enough of it to record it here, but even if I did, I could not replicate the Urdu accent with which we sang it for Shahid and Jane, in such celebration and gusto.

Yet now I must return, with some reluctance, to Islamabad and introduce you—dear reader—to Aunty Nuri. Aunty Nuri. She was not a biological aunt, but the wife of Pip's dear friend, Dr. Saeed (not to be confused with Dr Sadiq). He was a wonderful doctor, and I cannot describe the succor he gave me when he walked into my bedroom—I was laid up with the measles or flu or suchlike—carrying his brown leather doctor's bag and looking at me with such kind eyes. (What happened to doctors with kind eyes? Have they been computerized out of existence? Lost, maybe, in some compassionate conservatism?) But his wife was somewhat different. She had an energy that was most happy when it was interfering with someone else's business. That requires strength and imagination. It was Aunty Nuri, after all, who staged a reconciliation with the Brigardier's family and our own after Ifat's madcap runaway marriage. And it was she who, after my lovely's sudden demise, took it upon herself to reconcile us with Ifat's children. A foolish thought: what reconciliation did we need with those heart-torn children, except that Pip had put up the language of estrangement between us? So Aunty Nuri patted my hand and told me what I should say to my father. She spoke with a sweet, affectionate voice that had a somewhat slow drawl: "Sara *jani*, you just tell your papa, 'You are my *life*, you are my *joy*, you are my *peace*' . . ." I thought to myself that those were not exactly the epithets I would apply to Pip, but I listened. "And then you say," continued Aunty Nuri, " '*But!* You are a *dog*, you are a *cur*, to keep me from my sister's children!' " Nuri had now reached her triumphant conclusion. "Tell him, Sara dearest, 'YOU ARE A BITCH!' "

We didn't need to tell you anything, did we, Pip? Of course we went to see Ifat's children and enjoyed, painfully, our reencounter. But this was designed to be a secret, so that we could see the children and Pip should not be informed, and then life between us could continue quite merrily. Tillat's eldest boy, Omi, however, had different designs. I think he must have sensed an adult secret being enacted and chose to take control. "Nana [maternal grandfather]," he said in a voice as bright as a bell when Pip had returned from the Information Ministry or wherever else he was working, "Nana, we met our cousins today." Pip looked up. "Oh really?" he answered slowly. "Yes, Nana," continued Omi, "and they have such a big dog!" "Really," responded my father. Tillat and I were in the room and exchanged despairing glances. Omi went trotting out to some boyhood game, and then Pip turned to us. "Girls," he said ominously, "girls." That in itself should have been a sufficient reprimand. "I thought I told you that we did not want to have any further dealings with the Mawaz family?" "But, Pip," I groaned inside myself, "they are my sister's children; how can they be made responsible for her cruel, unuseful death?" Tillat and I, however, continued to look guilty for a crime that we had not committed. It was only years later that Ifat's children were admitted to Pip's household. That was in the Shahida era, when—to the children's great surprise—she was able to pinch each one on the cheek, burbling, "Shweet, shweet, so-so shweet!"

Listen, Pip. This is not a complaint. It is history. You were so hither and thither, so much back and forth, that it is hard for me to be chronological. In any case, my instincts have never led me to chronology. When I was in middle school, struggling with mathematics, my mother kindly said, "Why don't you ask Papa for some help with your homework?" I did, and what help it was. He looked with scorn at my long-division conundrum and then proceeded to say, "*Ek Bata Char, do bate theran, thin bate hazar,*" and this was in a rapid Punjabi. I did not speak Punjabi. "Don't you see how easy it is?" he yelled, casting my homework back toward me. "Oh, yes, Pip," I answered ruefully. "Very, very simple." Today I am somewhat glad that Pip is in his grave before he learned to master the computer. I can just see him bullying the Internet, and perplexing its systems, by punching in *"Ek Bata Char, do bate theran."* For punching was something Pip was apt to do.

He would punch people at airports, quite routinely. His family would be there to welcome him home on one of his frequent trips. (Why did we go each time, I wonder. Was it for affection?) Invariably, a lout in the waiting lounge would brush pass me or one of my sisters. Forget about Pip's luggage. He would lunge forth like a wild bull, assault the offender, and then declaim, "How dare you touch my daughter?" The punch delivered, Pip would become quite reasonable again, happy to chat to us about Dhaka or Vienna, or whichever city he had been in. We were embarrassed, both by the passing graze and by Pip's uncanny ability to divine its occurrence. I am sad to say that my sister Ifat inherited this habit, too. When out with her, Tillat and I would wonder if she knew how much she resembled Pip when she would turn upon our assailant, punch him, and then hiss, "How dare you touch my sister?"

Ifat wore rings, just as I do, so both of us are—or, were—equipped with aesthetic knuckle-dusters. I do not believe I have used mine in vain, but she certainly did. It was quite an astonishing shock to a passerby, when she—that tall, elegant woman—reached forth to deliver a punch that would have made Muhammad Ali quite proud. "How dare you touch my sister?" Ifat would proclaim, with no awareness of how her leopard skull began resembling a lion's head so much further from her own. No, I was not there when Ifat died, although in some strange way I think she dies inside me daily. Why should she leave our lives without a word, with no one there to say, "How dare you touch my sister?" She was gone by the time I returned to Lahore; she was quite gone. "Oh, my love, my love," Tillat whispered on my arrival, when we had the courage to meet each other's eyes.

And so it goes. When Pip died, I moaned. I thought some remnant in me had been discarded; I needed you to look at me and say, once again, with your unreplicated disgust, "You children." Then I turned away and considered different pastures new. Yes, you were in some other valley (Is heaven a valley? I have no idea) and the rest of us moaning, groaning, over your sweet remains. Then, a year or so later, Tillat rang me with the following news: "You know, Sara, Shahida has set up a trust fund." "Oh no!" I cried, fearing what would come next. "Yes, Sara, her home is now the Z. A. Suleri Trust House." "No," I moaned and groaned. "She has set up a Z. A. Suleri Trust; she is the president, but guess who is the vice president?" A chilly sensation seized my spine. "Don't tell me, don't tell me," I begged. But she did. "Sara Suleri Goodyear is the vice president!" I withered, just as a woman should, declaring fiercely that no one is entitled to use my name in vain. No use. Shahida is probably—even as we speak—making copies of everything I say for the Z. A. Suleri Trust Foundation. (Can there be such a thing as a Trust Foundation? I have no notion of such things.) Let her go on living, let her live well, while we live in the mercifully distant shadow of her exceptional sisterhood.

اپنی دنیا آپ پیدا کر، اگر زندوں میں ہے
اقبال

Give birth to your own world, if you are among the living!

— IQBĀL, *KHIZR-E-RAH*

For a man, Pip, you certainly gave continuous birth. I refer less to your offspring than to your newspapers, your projects. You always seemed to have something afoot, a bird in the bush and several more in hand. I thought perhaps you would mellow somewhat with age, but it never happened. After your first eye operation in Islamabad, when Ifat was in charge, a most remarkable doctor kept chanting to her, "No hurry! No worry!" That posed a twofold problem: of course his daughter would worry, and of course Pip was in a hurry to leave the hospital and return to whatever he was thinking of writing. And if not writing, then chiseling: no, Pip was not a stonemason in his spare time, but "chiseling" was his favorite word for the act of revision. It made my heart sink, after I had laboriously transcribed an article of his into legible handwriting, to watch him receive it with brief thanks and immediately proceed to chisel. He would chisel from dusk to dawn, and I, recipient of those shavings, would obediently rewrite page after page, para after para. No wonder I have such an adamantly different style of writing, when each word that I put down on paper is both my first and my last. "How remarkable," my friends tell me, but it isn't remarkable at all. It's Pip, the influence of Pip.

"You know, Sara," my friend Mehreen told me when she called from Florida, "I can't think of your father as anything else but Pip." And so she should. I first knew Mehreen at Presentation Convent in Rawalpindi: we were out of touch for years, nearly decades, until we accidentally met at some wedding in New York. Since then, it is safe to say that we have been in virtually daily contact. And she provides me with some memorable moments. Mehreen described, telephonically, the short-term impotence of her latest lover. "Well, it's easier for women," I responded, "for we can fake." "Fake?" replied Mehreen, never one to mince her words. "*Fake?* I deserve an Academy Award for my ability to fake!" And then she proceeded to tell me, with some indignation, that anything but the missionary position was illegal in Florida. (Please do not quote me on this issue, for I have no idea if it's true. I am merely recording a charming conversation.) "Illegal!" said Mehreen in protest, and then added as an afterthought—for she is a most honest woman when she is not lying—"I really don't mind. I am quite too lazy for anything else."

"Holy crow," Austin would say as he regarded her, "holy crow." He loved Mehreen when she visited us in Maine for some American holidays, both for what she was and for the obvious fact of how much I was devoted to her. But Austin's most famous "holy crow" has to be relegated to Italy. We had gone on a walking tour of Tuscany with Shahid and Jane, and some of those walking days turned out to be quite long. After sneering at my brand-new hiking boots and taking along his English leather walking shoes instead, Austin came to grief on one of our longest walks. For one thing, we got lost, but that didn't matter. What mattered was that his beloved shoes began to unravel, so that both shoes would clap like castanets, and at each clap Austin would mutter, "Holy crow, holy crow." We were on our way to the Villa Campestri, and the walk certainly took us up hill and down dale. Jane had gone on ahead in her bright fashion, and so Shahid, Austin, and I got seriously lost. I was trudging—no, I was hobbling—behind the two men when they paused to say, "Look, Sara! A restaurant!" It is true that amidst that isolated countryside we had suddenly come upon a restaurant, with crisp white tablecloths, waiters with white linen napkins poised upon their arms, and fatally inviting chairs. I knew both Shahid and Austin wanted to use me as an excuse to take a much-needed break, but I was undeterred. "How pretty," I said, barely glancing at the restaurant, and trudged some more along the straight and narrow. "Holy crow, holy crow," muttered Austin to my rear.

I think you would have been amused, Pip, by my first solitary encounter with Jinx Roosevelt, Austin's daughter and now my step. She is older than I am. But try to picture my delight when she said to me, most affectionately, "I knew Pop would remarry, but an intellectual! And—a nonwhite!" That's a nice phrase. If ever I am in arrears, or need to assert my virtue in some way, I say in my defense to Austin, "I am nonwhite." The Roosevelts welcomed me, although I think they expected Austin to return from his cruise with a matron rather than a Paki professor, but the surprise gradually wore off. Today, I would hazard a guess that Frank, Jinx's husband, is fonder of me than he is of Austin, but that is just a surmise. We certainly enjoy the time we spend with their children, a lovely brood, now producing broods of their own: it makes me feel quite proud of myself, to think that I have leapfrogged all intervening generations to achieve the accomplished status of step-great-grandmother. That, I think, is quite a feat.

Austin Goodyear. Anther, as Pip would say, another phenomenon. ("Anther" is Pip's rendition of "another": it has entered our vocabulary, has it not, Pip?) We met on a Yale-Harvard cruise, where I was a lecturer on an Ancient Silk Routes tour: I don't recall saying much about silk, but still, I talked. I had agreed to do it because I wanted a trip to Pakistan, where the boat was going. The cruise began in Bombay at precisely the time of unutterable sectarian violence that followed the destruction of the Babri Masjid in Ayodhya. How can people be so stupid? Who cares if the spot was in legend reputed to be the birthplace of Rama; who cares if Babur—a sweet emperor—chose to build a mosque upon it? Was its existence really significant enough to unleash such hatred that could destroy—never mind the mosque—so many human lives? I rather liked Babur. In his memoirs he bemoaned the fact that only in India did people eat grain with grain, wheat with wheat. It's true. And I am also impressed by the legend that claims that when in need of relaxation after a day's battle, Babur would tuck a willing soldier under each armpit and leap from battlement to battlement in order to soothe his soul. I like that. Not a habit that I would take up myself, of course, but one that does indicate a certain ingenuity of mind.

But back to the boat. Given the bloody violence in Bombay, the Yale-Harvard Alumni Association wisely decided to begin the cruise in Goa, and equally wisely, albeit apologetically, suggested that my Mozzi proclivities precluded my joining them in India. I think they had visions of headlines reading, "YALE PROFESSOR SLAIN IN BOMBAY! SHE WAS A MUSLIM!" or "GOAN POPULACE ATTACK YALE CRUISE SHIP! THE PROFESSOR WAS A MUSLIM!" In any case, it was fine by me, since it simply gave me a few more days in Karachi with my dear, dear brother-in-law Feroze. He and his friends always made a hospitable fuss of me, and in fact Feroze would charmingly say, after my departure, "I am suffering from P.S.S." P.S.S. equals Post-Sara Syndrome. I loved being taken care of and welcomed into any number of homes, although I really wasn't prepared for Abdul. Feroze warned me about his friend, "He sings." Halfway through the dinner party given in my honor, Abdul burst into song and continued singing well into the night. "Abdul," I was finally constrained to say, "I have never seen anyone give so generously of their lack of talent."

And how the Karachi-ites shrieked with laughter when they heard of the itinerary the Ivy League had designed for its unsuspecting cruise group, a so-called tour of Karachi! A bus ride to Jinnah's mausoleum and a trip to the Karachi National Museum, an edifice of which I had never heard and was no poorer for such lack of knowledge. "You should have given us some notice and brought the group here!" cried Naheed and Kamal Azfar in their lovely home in Clifton. "We would have loved to entertain them!" They would, for they are good at such things, but it was too late. Instead, I found myself joining the group and contemplating the ramshackled artifacts in the Karachi National Museum. I made a quick getaway and took solace in a cigarette outside the bus. A member of the group approached me. He was tall and bald. "You shouldn't smoke," he said. "My wife died of lung cancer last year, and it really isn't a good idea." Who is this person, I thought, to accost me thusly? Should I attempt to pull my rank on him? I didn't, because he was older than me, but did take a quick look at his Yale alumni name tag. There I read, fatefully, "Austin Goodyear."

Why had I never got married? Interesting point. On an average scale, I do believe I am desirable, and nice enough too, on top of that. But marriage was the fate in Pakistan from which I had to run away, and during my American sojourn, no one in the States quite made sense to me. I was about to turn forty in a month or two, although my decision, I think, came after. I recall an evening in Egypt, in Luxor, after a breathtaking day at the tombs, when Austin approached me with some hesitation to ask if I was going to return to the tombs to see a son et lumière display that same evening. "Certainly not!" I replied. "I've been there all day and the last thing I want to do is go back to have people flashing lights at me and playing what they think are ancient Egyptian chants! No, I am going to take a stroll by the Nile." It struck Austin as a good idea too, and so he joined me, in every sense of the word.

And I did take up his offer; I did visit him in Maine, staying in the little guest room that Tillat, my heart's ease, will shortly inhabit. I liked him, yes, of course, but I did not expect to find him as extraordinary as I did. Perhaps it was his language. Would I be his special friend, he asked: I was touched, because it seemed so quaint, and I did not want to ask— even gently—"And what does *that* entail?" By the next time I visited, I was told, "There is an *important letter* waiting next to your dinner plate." I opened it with curiosity, to respond with profound astonishment. It was a premarital agreement, all done up in legalese, duly signed by Austin and his lawyer, leaving a little virgin space for me to sign! I laughed as heartily as I had for many a year and said, "All right, I'll do it. Only you'd better hurry up and make all the arrangements before I change my mind," I added warningly. Needless to say, Austin hurried, and within a couple of days or so, we were wed.

Before that time, I had turned forty in Tunis. It was during one of those peculiar conferences that we never really knew the title of before we arrived, but we went anyway, Geoffrey and Renee Hartman, Paul Fry, our student Ian, and myself. Most of the proceedings were conducted in Arabic and French, spoken rapidly, and I can claim facility in neither language. So we just sat there and looked solemn, privately agreeing that it really didn't matter that we didn't know the title of the conference, since we couldn't understand a word of the talks anyway. But we loved the sea; we loved the food; and Geoffrey is particularly good at giving sagacious nods during a lecture he would be hard-pressed to paraphrase. And our cordial hosts did not seem to mind our ignorance at all: it was as though they had staged the event to include "Enter—Silent Yale Chorus."

Those conferences. I'm glad I do them with less frequency these days, because sometimes a flash of common sense would descend upon the participants' jet-lagged faces, imprinting an expression that clearly read, "Why am I doing this? Is the profession so important? Why have I traveled so many miles for this?" Think of Moscow. Yes, I was very happy to be in the city itself, but all those hours in a conference room! Hugh Kenner and I were the only participants who spoke no Russian: we were handed headphones to listen to simultaneous English translation of the speeches, but the headphones didn't work. They either made particularly shrill electronic shrieks into our ears, or we would catch a word or two in English amidst ten beeps. One sentence, however, came across loud and clear, one that I will never forget. It was the final talk of the final day of the conference, and a young, rather trendy novelist was having his say. We listened: "You can dig yourself a grave six feet deep and find your grandmother in it." Maybe there is a profundity to the phrase that I still can't see, but it moved me to considerable merriment, and I escaped to chuckle my chortles in the crisp Moscow air. And, reader, you are lucky: I will not even begin to describe the symposium in Berlin.

But now I must get back to Brooklin. Think how I felt eight years ago when Paul and Mary and when Linda awkwardly welcomed my incongruous entry into this household: through thick and thin, the latter has been my dear friend ever since. Yet how was I to convey this trans-mogrification to you, my Pip? I told you over the telephone, and here is another way in which Shahida can be remarkably useful. She imme-diately assumed that I was now sitting on an inordinate tire fortune, and henceforth would address me—with a coy smile—as "Sara-Begum-Sahiba!" Austin wrote the sweetest letter to Pip, as an introduction to himself. As he sat down to write, I proffered some ginger words of cau-tion: try not to dwell too much upon your age, I advised, and not too much upon your prior marriage. Austin must have misheard, I think, because he proceeded to do precisely that. Oh dear, I thought to myself, oh dear. After quite a glaring lapse of time, Pip actually responded. It was a brief letter, written in his neatest handwriting: "Sara is a wonder-ful woman, and she is my favorite child." (Now, Shahid, Tillat, Irfan, please don't get choosy as you read that sentence. You know very well that Pip—permeable as he was—would have written exactly the same about each of you had the occasion arisen. It didn't, and by sheer chance, I became its recipient. No worry, no hurry. Please.) "Yours, Z.A.S." Since A.G. likes initials, he must have warmed to the Z.A.S., but he did not see the P.S. so clearly redolent for me that read, in invisible ink, "Sara, make him a Muslim!"

Oh my tenderhearted boy, Z. A. Suleri, how you would have suffered for your sons at the time of your funeral! It was Shahid who told me, time and again, "I could not have done without Farooq in those days." Farooq, Tillat's husband, was there with Shahid, specially for the process I do not wish to imagine, the ritual bathing of the corpse. Farooq said to me, "Do you know how small Papa was?" I had not thought about that, but it was true. "When I held him in my arms to wash the body," Farooq told me, "I could not believe that he was so small. You see," he added, "there was so much presence to him; he always struck you as larger-than-life." Yes, he did, I mused, that lion's head, with its outrageous posture of surprise. Why did Pip look so perpetually astonished? I remember him declaiming about Muslim nationhood; getting astonished at every-one's stupidity; laughing heartily at each of his own jokes; expressing amazement any time one of his children did something that displeased him, which was often. Yes, I remember. And I remember you, Papa.

But now I must get back to Brooklin. I knew in our early courtship that Austin had a yacht that he loved most passionately—possibly more than me, I imagine. She was not in the water during my first few trips to Maine, but when she was, what a surprise lay in store for me. *Mermaid* is her name, *Mermaid*, and this old farmhouse in Maine is cluttered, everywhere, with every known representation of mermaids that could be conceived. There are statues of mermaids on the rocks, mermaids on the walls, mermaids on the pillows, mermaids on the stationery. I thought it was quite charming, and when Austin invited me out for a sail, I thought that was charming, too. I had often gone sailing in the Karachi harbor and at Brighton too, smiling benignly at the crew while we lolled upon the decks. Little did I know. On this excursion, the configuration was slightly different. The crew, *c'est moi*. I was the crew.

Please keep in mind, dear reader, that I do not know how to drive. Let alone a car, I have never been able to master a bicycle. In fact, I was even a little weak-kneed on a tricycle. The only machine of impulsion I have been able to master is a scooter: please do not mistake me, because I certainly don't mean a scooter of the motorized variety. The one on which I was most confident was a little metal thing that I could scoot off with one foot, along the pavements of London. That little scooter was a friend of mine, a present, I believe, for my eighth birthday. So understand the terror that struck my soul when we mounted *Mermaid* (mounted is not the right word, but it will do) and Austin said to me, "You take the helm." I did, but my knuckles were white and my brow was wet. I had no idea that I was designed to be Ancient Mariner to Austin's Coleridge, but it turns out that is exactly what I was primed to be. A sense of direction has never been my finest point, and I must say it turned doubly difficult when I had to deal with a completely novel terminology, such as "port," "starboard," and any number of etceteras. And Austin could not control his shouting. "Ready about!" he would scream at me. "Heartily!" I love to be hearty, but when I don't know exactly what I am meant to be hearty about, it causes some problems. On their visit shortly after our marriage, Shahid and Jane were sitting on the deck, smiling at me compassionately, as I manned the helm. "But, my darling, you're shaking!" Austin said as he returned from some complexity with the mizzen. "Why?" I responded, with a tinge of bitterness. "It really is quite simple. I am shaking because you have been shouting at me, that's all."

Austin's friends would ask him, when he announced his unlikely marriage, "Is she a sailor?" Unfortunately, I am not. There are so many failings to which I should confess that I don't mind including sailing as one of them. I was never particularly good at football (the English version, soccer, I suppose), I was tolerable at badminton, and in our cricket games, I was perfectly happy to serve as mate to Shahid's captain. (Mate? Have I hit upon the word most appropriate? Doesn't it have a suspiciously nautical ring to it?) But what wonderful cricket matches our family held on our lawns in Lahore, Pip, beautifully sunny winter afternoons when you'd actually leave your writing and come out to have a game with us! Of course, you remained preposterous. There was a very engaging bank of sweet peas at one side of our garden, pushing their tendrils through a delicate bamboo trellis, colorful and sweet smelling. That was strictly off-limits. If one of us, as a batting team, accidentally hit our pitch into the sweet peas, Pip was there as an umpire, to say: "Foul shot, foul shot." When he was batting, however, and sent our leather cricket ball straight into the sweet peas, "*Chika*," he would declare triumphantly, "a sixer!" Because Pip was perfectly comfortable with being unfair with his children: if they bruised a sweet pea, they were out; if he sent down a cascade of flowers and bamboo latticework, he was the winner. Mamma just sat there, shaking her head at us, in a winter garden in Lahore.

I'm glad you won your games, Pip. It does not make sense that you should lose so very many. On that score, at least, you and Austin have something in common—it could be me—and I think of it each time when I take the helm of *Mermaid* and head out away from you into the waters of Eggemoggin Reach rather than the Indian Ocean.

میرے دین و مذہب کواب پوچھتے کیا ہو اُن نے تو
قشقہ کھینچا، دَیر میں بیٹھا، کب کا تَرک اسلام کیا
میر

Why ask about Mir's religion and beliefs?
He has long since drawn a line on his forehead,
sat in a temple, and renounced Islam

— MĪR TAKI MĪR

*T*here was a time when we would go to the open-air theater in Lawrence Gardens in Lahore, where—before Islamization set in with a ven-
geance—they would hold miraculous nightlong musical festivals, and
you could listen to Begum Akhtar singing Faiz and Ghālib, Iqbal Bano
doing something similar, and then the Sabri Brothers themselves. It is
hard to describe a *quawwali* to the uninitiated. The music is Sufi, no-dort,
mystical, passionate, opening in a low key, and then rising in crescendo
after crescendo to evocations that cause its audience literally to do a

swaying dance in response to its lovely cadences. This is, of course, in an era before the stupid nonsense that has set up such fierce barriers between Sunni and Shia in Islam: no, Sunnis though we may have been, tears coursed down our cheeks as we listened to the Sabris sing, "And that lovely grandchild of Muhammad's, / Whose neck was cut as he knelt in prayer." In fact, I have often wished to have mastered the clap of a good *quawwali* group, beginning almost as though hands were preparing for slow prayer, and then moving among the intricacies of that music into almost a frenetic beat, impossible to resist. I remember Ifat and Tillat looking at me with restrained alarm when in Islamabad, during Tillat's first pregnancy, I suddenly began clapping and singing, "Oh, midwife Halima, in your lap, the moon is coming to descend!" Halima was Muhammad's (peace) midwife, and Sufi music makes as much of his birth as the average Christmas-farer does of Christ's.

But there is clapping and then there is clapping. On our most recent trip, sitting in one of those draining airport lounges, Austin and I were biding our time until a diminutive African American lady came up and asked if the seat beside us was vacant. I immediately removed my bag and politely responded, "Yes." She sat down next to me and began to clap. "What is she doing?" whispered Austin to me. "She's clapping," I whispered back. "Maybe she really wanted that seat." How wrong I was. "Hallelujah!" she began chanting, in a voice strong enough to belie the size of her body. "HALLELUJAH!" She told us that God had spoken to her at 5:00 A.M. that morning and said she must go down to O'Hare Airport at Gate B-4 to tell the sinners how to cleanse their souls. "Can't it be six?" she chatted back to God, but apparently He was adamant. Since I was the closest sinner sitting next to her, I tried to look sufficiently penitent. But that was not enough. She held forth with increasing vociferation, and I think I kept my calm until I saw the expressions of newcoming passengers entering the gate. They would stop, astonished, and stare at our roaming airport preacher, then hastily take a seat as far away from her as possible. "LAUGH!" the little lady screamed at me. "LAUGH! But not the laugh of a sinner! Laugh in praise of the Lord!" Luckily our flight was on time, and God beamed down an injunction that His messenger might have better luck at Gate B-5.

I don't know. It must be in our genes. I know that I at least have the most uncannily bad luck in attracting zombies. It doesn't matter if it is a human being, or a virulent mosquito wedded to a black fly, or a mad dog. With a deadly and unerring instinct, they find me. And I am happy to admit that I am terrified of zombies. What if their aura is contagious; what if I woke up—like Professor Challenger—with a strong need to bite a perfectly innocent maid on the calf or thigh? That's from *The Poison Belt*. I think every one should study that wonderfully cautionary tale. I even suggested to Shoshana that we try to fit it into our Judgment and Forgiveness seminar, somewhere between *The Cenci* and Oscar Wilde, but it would not cohere. Never mind, next time, we said, for I do believe we will be teaching that course forever: it could be an oasis, perhaps, far away from Yale, where the only available zombie would be me.

Well, Pip, you certainly didn't give equal attention to such learning. Your madcap schemes were quite inexorable, almost as though you were in collusion with the zombies who desired to infect me with their zombie-dom. Pip had a plan, on one of our holiday Himalayan trips, to bring back one of those mountain people from the hills and train him to be a bearer. "They are so loyal!" Pip said in absolute confidence—he must have been reading Kipling—"loyal, loyal, loyal!" We looked askance, but there was no stopping him. So before we knew it, the Valley View Hotel personnel had helped us find such a lad, and to say he was uncouth would be a gentle euphemism.

He (I believe Aslam was his name) traveled back with us to Rawalpindi and took up residence with us. He was not exactly trainable. For example, he would take four hours off in the morning to go and urinate. "Where were you?" my mother would demand when he returned. "Urinating," Aslam would reply in a slightly simpering manner. "What!" said my mother—and here her remarkable Urdu cannot be replicated—"which human being do you know who needs four hours to urinate? Aren't we short enough of water as it is?"

A rhetorical claim that demands some elucidation. After the '65 war there was a considerable water shortage in West Pakistan, which meant that we had to get a military water truck to stop by whenever they could to pump water into our upstairs and downstairs tanks and pray that it would last until all of us had performed our necessary ablutions. At an undetermined, unspecified time of the day, however, the regular taps would begin to hiss and spit out water, at which moment all of us would be in a tizzy trying to fill buckets, cauldrons, saucepans, and any receptacle that could hold the blessed water. Aslam's job was to go to the farthest garden tap and fill up the buckets: his task provided us with a dizzying sentence that I do not believe has an equal. "Tired filling water-water, tired filling water-water," Aslam would declaim. If Pip was at home writing, the idea of loyalty to his order had left him: "Shut up, Aslam," Pip would plead, or, rather, snarl most ferociously. But that young mountain lad had a spirit of his own. "Tired filling water-water," he would keep chanting; if anything, his voice rising as the buckets were filled. And all of us now, whether I am writing or Shahid is painting or Tillat is packing, simply say to one another to convey our true state of mind, "Tired filling water-water." Aslam did not bestow his inefficiency on us for too long: he went for a vacation back to the mountains and decided, without a word to us, not ever to return. Very loyal, those hill men are—about as loyal as those monkeys sitting in their trees primed to snatch away each morsel if your hand is not vigilant.

Monkeys. Recall the times, Pip, when you would mercilessly tease your son Shahid when he was about four or five by telling him his mother was a monkey, that she had come up to him in Nathia Gali one summer. "Take this baby monkey of mine back with you to the plains," Pip claims the mother monkey said, "for I can't stand him anymore." The sad part about that silly oft-repeated joke was the truth that even at four, my brother both knew its imaginative zest and its sad implication: Why is my father rejecting me, his small face said. For, Pip, although you were one to cavort, even you would not cavort with monkeys. I recall at three seeing Pip place Shahid boisterously on a fruit tree outside our home, declaring, "Shahid! Your mother the monkey wants to visit you! We'll see you later! Good-bye!" I recall looking up at my brother, his legs dangling, his chin a-wobble. (We were always prone to wobbling chins; it might have been the Celtic genes in us, who knows. Tears can accumulate in the chin and make it most irrational. I know Tillat wobbled, and I wobbled. Maybe we still do: who knows.)

But what an outrageous lie it is to claim that children, close to infants, do not know what rejection is or what the state of compassion may be! They may lack the vocabulary but not the complexity, as I think I knew when I stared up at Shahid with fear and compassion, neither of us certain whether his neglected posture of half a minute would end with the return of my father or whether his monkey mother would actually arrive.

Avaunt. I will not dwell upon that generational, obsessional teasing among us, largely generated by you, Pip. So there is no need to linger upon such similar stories as Ifat in cahoots with her fairy godmother to make herself into a witch; Sara selling her golden singing voice for a mingy pot of gold; or Shahid himself entering with gusto into prolonged stories about how Tillat's nose was bitten off by a wolf or a raven—something carnivorous—and how Irfan's mother was certainly a monkey. And where was Mamma amidst all this? Could she not have intervened to say something like "A foolish joke, a foolish joke" or "Boys, you know I am your mother. Your mother was not a monkey"? Maybe she thought we were of such hardy stock, we did not need such comforting. I think we did, although the last thought in my mind is to raise such recriminations with my ghosts. Tired filling water-water. I have had enough to do with monkeys.

"Enough to do with monkeys!" I exclaimed in Costa Rica, where a very diligent and energetic guide was beckoning Austin, urging me through the splendors of the rain forest. Indeed, it was splendid, but after ten hours I had had enough and parked myself on a tree stump in the pathway. "Just one more hour's walk, and then maybe we will get to see some howling monkeys!" urged our guide. "I can hear them howl," I replied sourly but I hope not impolitely. "Isn't that enough?" Apparently it wasn't, for he went rushing off into the verdant undergrowth in the hopes of manipulating the howlers in my direction. Luckily, it did not work. Shortly thereafter, however, the guide came scurrying back, with a look of triumph on his face. "Sara, Sara, come with me!" "Why?" I asked. "I can show you a boa constrictor giving birth to a baby! Pregnant boa constrictor! Just a few yards down the path!" For some reason I knew I was not delighted that such a reptile was in close vicinity to the place of my repose. Neither was I particularly thrilled to conceive of it in the act of progeneration. "Your description of it is exhilarating enough," I responded kindly. "Why don't you sit down and tell me about the birds?" There were, as it turned out, nothing but sparrows around us at that spot. "A sparrow!" I exclaimed. "A sparrow! How interesting, how interesting!" The guide looked at me with dubiety, which only increased when I couldn't help but add, "There's a special providence in the fall of a sparrow. . . . The readiness is all." Horatio to my Hamlet, he could not help mutter an excuse and wander off, to where the boa constrictor was absenting itself from felicity.

That was your habit, Pip, you know, to return from the Gymkhana Club and say, "Sara, read me some *Hamlet*!" or: "Read me 'Ballad of Reading Gaol'!" I think I enjoyed that better than listening to your prognostications about world affairs and what the government would do next, but it became a trifle painful when your next demand would be, "Now play me the Russian birdsong record!" That was hard. On each of his official trips, Pip would return with an odd assortment of official gifts: Beijing brought us back more Red Books than we knew what to do with, although Moscow was both more eclectic and perplexing. Why a jolly Russian wench doll, with a tea cozy tucked where other things should be? And why a record, titled *Famous Birdsongs of the USSR*? I am not averse to chirrups, but they belong elsewhere than to a long-playing record. The coos would begin quite prettily, but then degenerate into squawks, followed by some strange rustling sounds interrupted by slow moans. "Beautiful," Pip would say, "beautiful." But then he had strange notions. On his return from Brussels once, it was clear he was glad to be home, when he suddenly exclaimed, "What a piece of work is man!" For some reason, he was staring at the Kashmiri walnut coffee table in front of him. I was expecting a disquisition on European politics, but that was a mistake. Instead, Pip ran his finger across the table and murmured almost to himself, "What artifice, what ingenuity." Then he surprised us all by looking up to proclaim, "Consider this table. Think of the labor, the artisanship, that allows some noble men in those lovely mountains to collect walnut shells and grind them into a texture like this!" Taken aback, I said, "But, Pip, there are no shells involved, this—" "This," he interrupted mildly, "is a walnut table. There are noble men who must grind the shells, and then chisel them—just as I do my writing—into surfaces as smooth as this!" "But, Pip," I tried repeating, "the walnut is a *tree*. That's where the wood comes from, its bole and limbs and whatever else is woody, but certainly not from its nuts." Pip waved me away in a dismissive change of subject, but later in the evening I think I heard him mutter, "Oh: a walnut is a tree."

You would have been saddened, Pip, to learn of the death of Malika-e-Tarannum, the Queen of Melody, Nur Jehan. What an institution she was. She was originally known as Baby Nur Jehan, then the respectful term Bebe, and kept the apellation well into her fifties, until the Paki government honored her with the title Queen of Melody. I believe she started her career as a film actress in pre-partition days but soon came to be valued more for her voice than her body. By the time I was old enough to recognize her, she was grotesquely beautiful, a woman larger-than-life. While Ifat and I were students at Queen Mary College in Lahore (it really is a girls' school), Nur Jehan had a daughter attending it as well, and so would graciously donate her time to come and put on makeup for the little girls before their annual play. What an occasion that was. We children would line up outside the staff room in which the grand lady had been installed with an impressive array of lipstick, powder, and paint. One by one we'd enter to be held firmly between her prodigious and sari-clad knees, our chins grasped in one bejeweled hand, while the Queen of Melody would with remarkable speed spray-paint our faces. "Next!" she would call out commandingly, tossing an emptied red rouge jar over her shoulder. "Next!" I remember when the annual play was a pastoral horticultural pageant, and I was waiting for my turn in my white crepe-paper daisy costume. When I left looking like a small whorelet to join the other little girls who had received the Nur Jehan treatment, I was very glad that I had been chosen to be a daisy rather than a poppy. We went into the staff room with some innocence and emerged dripping with experience.

A remarkable woman. And not all the facelifts in Switzerland—of which she had several—could mitigate her strength of character. There was a range to her voice: it could be intelligently pure, as when she sang *ghazal*s by Faiz; quite rollicking and jolly when she turned to spirit-stirring patriotic war songs; and then earthy, husky, when she sang singularly erotic Punjabi love songs. There was a range to other aspects of her life, too. Khalid Hasan, the journalist, wrote a piece on Nur Jehan—and this was during her lifetime—that described her holding court with a group of her admirers. They were affectionately asking her how many lovers she had had, suggesting names, and enjoying her bantering denials. Joining in the fun, she finally said, "Oh! After all my 'no's,' we've already reached seventeen!" You would recall Khalid Hasan, Pip, for he worked with you, as did Omar Kureishi: apart from Kureishi's cricket commentator voice on Radio Pakistan, he was also renowned for the puckish wit in the pieces he wrote for you when you edited the *Times of Karachi*.

How strangely that fact was brought back to me some years ago at Yale. The young filmmaker Hanif Kureishi had been invited to campus to give a lecture on his work, and I—as the resident Paki—had been trotted out to introduce him before his speech. Hanif was young, dressed artistically in black, but curiously and sweetly enough had brought his father with him. Mr. Kureishi Senior, brimming with pride, was seated next to me in the front row. Even as the lecture began, he conducted a whispered conversation with me. Did I know his brother the cricket commentator? I nodded. Was I related to Z. A. Suleri, the editor? "His daughter." "How wonderful!"—as though this were an accomplishment of mine. "Do you know that I introduced your uncle Shams to your aunty Bertie?" I beamed. "How are they?" "Divorced." "Oh, what a tragedy, what a tragedy! And where is dear Shams?" "Deceased," I replied apologetically. Mr. Kureishi Senior expressed his regret in a series of suppressed "Oh's," and by now the audience was turning around to locate the source of these sibilant interruptions of Hanif's address. Senior was silent for a while, but then turned to me again. "And how is your dear mother?" he whispered chattily. My dear mother had been long since in her grave, but I did not dare distress Senior into more audible expressions of condolence. "Fine," I nodded reassuringly.

Pip was most amused when I told him this tale: for one, he loved to listen to me talk, and then was always astonished by the fact I know full well: whatever continents may intrude to interrupt our narrative, the circle of life only seems to grow tighter and tighter. Sometimes I feel that there will be no more strangers in my daily existence, but only remembrances, reminders. It is like the fragrance of sweet peas on the kitchen table, which can never be simply itself, but a shocking command into memory. For whatever has transpired, or will transpire, why do I always think of us as a bunch of children exceptionally given to joy?

It made me happy to listen to the little joke that Shahid told me, now more than a few years ago. He was walking briskly to the Green Park branch in London, where he was bank manager, when passing a bookshop he thought he saw my book smiling at him in the window. As a consequence, at lunchtime he rang up his friends and announced, "Sara's book is out! This calls for celebration! This calls for a liquid lunch!" His friends responded with alacrity, and some hours later one of them grew maudlin and suggested they go to look at Sara's book. I am sure it was Shahid Hyat. (Hyat, spouse of dear Sobia, who is sister of dear Laila, who is mother of my Ismael: such lists are endless.) They all thought it a splendid idea and went trooping off to the bookshop in liquid anticipation. And there they found not Sara at all, whose book would not be out for months, but—*Salad Days*, by Douglas Fairbanks.

Quite recently, I asked Tillat if the open-air theater in Lahore had been functioning in her time, and when she said no, we pondered over how many different Lahores we had known. Hers was the most startling: on her last trip to Lahore, she had stayed in a hotel, a daughter without a father, a child without a home. She had returned with a close friend, Farah, and was able to see Lahore through her eyes, almost as though she were a visitor, which is not a bad thing to do. After Pip's funeral, Shahid declared that this in all probability would be the last time he would return to Lahore; I devoutly hope the same is not true for me. For I plan to return, somehow, sometime, preferably with a companion, but if not, then on my own. I listened to Tillat tell me how she winced with compassion when, in the last years of her life, they went to Albert Hall to hear Nur Jehan sing. The face had been lifted; the voice had not. The Queen of Melody groped for her erstwhile passionate voice and could only reproduce shadows, torn tendrils of it.

You would have been moved, Pip, to hear Tillat telling Farooq that after you had died, the one extraordinary thing that she had lost was the complete surety of the joy she could confer by simply walking into a room. It is true, Pip: when one of us walked into your room, you would look up with such a radiance in your face, one that asked for nothing, nothing but the joy of presence. It was a very profound compliment that you conferred, which, however life enriching, was also curiously humbling. With humility we approached you, which is another way of expressing the joy we too were feeling, to be once again in the aura of your remarkable presence.

دوست یہاں کم ہیں اور بھائی بہت
حالی

There are many brothers here, but few friends

— H A L I

What was it about Pip's relationship to friends? He was a most affectionate man, quick both to love and to admire, yet I do not recall a single of his friendships that was not somehow trammeled by history. But then he had my mother. On one of my later trips to Lahore, I was sitting with him as he lay propped up in bed (he was beginning to spend more and more time in bed) and was expatiating about Mamma. I recollected rising in the morning and going down to the front veranda: the dew was still wet on the lawn and the two of them just sat there, sipping their scalding tea and reading the morning newspapers. There was an intangibly old intimacy about them then that made me smile. "Yes," I responded to the supine Pip years later, "yes, you were good friends." And I was startled by the gratitude with which he sat up and said, "Oh yes, Sara, thank you, Sara, oh yes, we were such good friends!"

Toward his children, however, Pip maintained a more ambivalent rigidity. We were encouraged to have friends, but not too many; they were welcome to visit our home, but not too often. Furthermore, it seems that each of us invariably had, in Pip's eyes, one good friend (welcome) and one bad friend (distinctly unwelcome). It would have been simple if the good/bad dichotomy remained stable but it did not, so we were never sure when we got up each day whether good had transmogrified into bad or the other way round in Pip's colorful emotional kaleidoscope. It was quite perplexing when Pip, after having close to banished one of our friends, would say affectionately some weeks later, "Where is X? I haven't seen him for ages! Has he forgotten us?" No, Pip, I thought then and do again today, you are not to be forgotten.

But to conceive of Pip himself as a friend instead of a father, we must go back into his boyhood and early manhood. There was his cousin Uncle Shamim and later the younger cousin Uncle Nasim, and with both men his relations were very different. (There was much-loved Uncle Jaffar, too, but that is another story.) He dearly loved Shamim and told us wonderful stories of how Shamim was convinced that Pip was the greatest writer of the twentieth century (both in Urdu and English, I believe). They stalked round Delhi and Bombay from editor to editor, with Shamim carrying manuscripts like a chalice and Pip following with the air of one too burdened by his own genius. One editor listened to them through with patience, ruffled through the typescripts Shamim had solemnly placed upon his desk, and said in kindness, "All right. I'll print this poem in the next anthology." "And what will you pay?" demanded Shamim. "Pay!" said the astonished editor. "Why—nothing!" "Then you can't have it," said Shamim with great affront. He snatched away the poem, gathered up the papers, and the two of them walked out, penniless but proud.

During my lifetime, I have watched Pip and Uncle Shamim roar with laughter as they reminisced about Shamim's role as a fledgling literary agent. I loved the man: there was a gentleness to his being beyond his obvious affection for his cousin Zia, and he was also very courteous toward my mother. Mair, he would call her, Mair, and never by her adopted Muslim name, Surraya. "How wonderful to have you back in Karachi, Mair, how well you look," Shamim would say. And then turning to me: "Sara! You imp! Are you going to grow up to be as sparkling as your mother?" It was a happy place to be, but then a gradual change set up between those two friends, who seemed to allow distances to well up between them. It was never as categorical as a falling-out, but more a retreat into several different silences. For one thing, Shamim lived in Karachi and we were here, there, and everywhere. More significant, I think, was the fact that politics entered the picture with its usual crude muddying of the delicacy of relations. Pakistan was busy creating another minority (with so many there already, why did they need one more?) and was turning its talons on to the Qadiani community, the Muslim sect to which my uncle belonged. And while I am relieved to say that Pip never joined the shameful movement to declare the group—legally and constitutionally—"non-Muslim," he did indeed write against the community that was his erstwhile home. So the two men adopted silence almost in deference to the distances between them. Shamim died betimes, and while Pip wept, he did not go to the funeral. Pip was never a great one for funerals.

Uncle Nasim, Shamim's younger brother: now that's a different story. He was considerably younger than my father, and in fact came to stay with Pip in London during the war, when Pip was ferociously engaged in the struggle for the Pakistan movement. Nasim and his brother could not have been more different, with one a trifle abrasive where the other was understated; one in perpetual suspicion where the other was most mild. And Nasim was the first to admit to being abrasive: one of his favorite phrases was "and then I lost my shirt." I remember him coming to lunch in Lalazar after the '65 war, recounting the saga of a tedious journey from London. I was impressed. During that trip—according to his own narration—Uncle Nasim must have lost his shirt at least fifteen times. It is lucky that he had a considerable wardrobe. He also told us that when in Karachi he could not possibly stay with friends or relatives because of the water shortages and because he could not stand "this *balti* [bucket] business." This was in the Aslam era, when buckets were very much in our mode. After a fine lunch, Nasim retired to the bathroom to wash his hands. "Go and help Uncle Nasim with his *balti* business," I whispered to Ifat, and we both collapsed into our hidden secrets of laughter.

I have an affection for Uncle Nasim, although shall never claim that there was anything like an intimate or a comfortable friendship between my father and him. For one thing, there was politics and all the sibling rivalries that it engenders: Uncle Nasim chose to follow in Pip's footsteps and also decided on journalism as his profession, albeit of a very different ilk. He essentially stayed in London and was a columnist and a television personage there, married to his Dutch wife, the artist Tiné. (Odd, how many men in my father's family have sought out European spouses. There's Pip, there's Shams with Swiss Bertie, Nasim with Dutch Tiné, and I do believe that there are more. We will not mention Shahid.) Politically, Nasim regarded himself as "left of center" and would look at my father as though he were an antediluvian object to be patronized, which irked my father considerably. Yet they stayed in touch, although over the years Uncle Nasim did seem to grow more self-satisfied inside his shirts. I certainly do not wish to seem harsh—I last saw Nasim when he was the Paki ambassador to the UN and he asked me to come to visit them in New York. This was shortly after Nuzzi's death, and Nasim was gentler, far more affectionate than he had ever been. When Nuzzi's brother-in-law Iqbal Akhund also came over for dinner, Nasim asked him of me, "Who does she remind you of?" "Need you ask?" replied Iqbal quietly. Ah God, I thought to myself, must my face always be an elegy for those dearly beloved, can it never be just itself? Vain thought. But I was glad that Nasim was so gentle with me, and even asked with what seemed to be genuine care about my father. "I am concerned about his health," he said, which Nasim really shouldn't have been, because he himself died the following month of a sudden heart ailment. "So Uncle Nasim lost his shirt one final time," Shahid said to me from London, meditatively. Yes, he had, and I sorrowed for how my world was being depopulated, and for my new friendship with this potential friend of Pip's.

So much for friends within the clan, a clan reft, of course, with the ravagement of the divorce through which Pip had left his first wife, Baji, his cousin, in a family tree far too complicated for me to clamber into. Tillat should be asked: I can attest that she climbed trees and performed all kinds of precarious physical acts that I was too nervous to contemplate. What I think I discern in Pip's vocabulary was a slow substitution for the term "friends" with the term "ally." He had befriended and had been befriended by any number of allies, but in his latter decades it was almost as though alliance and disalliance became his modus operandi, a phrase that continually cropped up in his editorials and articles. For a while, Bhutto seemed his greatest friend, and Farooq reminds me that Pip's icon—his cigar—was generated by his friendship with Bhutto. But that too fell apart, and (as I have written elsewhere) the politician was able to say to the editor, quite charmingly, "Ah, Z.A., Z.A. Now all we have in common is our initials."

No wonder we children have to reconsider the course of contact, where love becomes as ephemeral as a change of government. As I have said, Pip loved his friends, but somehow they seemed to be subjected to a five-year plan review, so one was never certain of their constancy. All allies had to be scrutinized—all, that is, except for Dr. Sadiq. He was no relative and thus exempt from the vagaries of family romances; neither was he a politician or a newspaper man, so there were no easy methods of establishing a parting of the ways with him. No, their seventy-year friendship went on intact, from the boyhood days when they ran together down the breathtaking hills of Simla, to the heart-wrenching day when Dr. Sadiq died. There was only one point when their friendship seemed endangered, and for once it had nothing to do with which government was or was not in power. It had to do with me.

I have told you, Pip, haven't I, that you were preposterous? Dr. Sadiq—a tall, handsome man with a kindly face—had two sons. His dearest friend, you, Pip, happened to have a daughter. The law of nature in Pakistan cried out that the bond between the two men should, most happily, be cemented in the wedlock of their offspring. It was not the bricks and mortar that I desired as my fate, so I had to work hard to break out of the edifice they were constructing for me. I have written about this before, but like all trauma, it deserves repetition. Why, Pip, why, you who could talk to me about every aspect of Muslim nationhood, *why* did you not consult me about the fact that Dr. Sadiq had been proposing such an alliance between our households? I was blissfully unaware of this proposition, while Pip responded telephonically to Sadiq, "On my part, brother, you can have her. But now you must ask the girl." You see, Pip was a politician, for his statement did not seem to infringe upon my rights at all, except that by all Paki standards of interpretation it would register as a resounding consent, with the formality of asking the little girl herself a frivolous ritual of finality. Dr. Sadiq would come from Karachi to Lahore—he hated traveling, so it must have been quite onerous—with a diamond ring in his pocket, to speak to the girl, who would be appropriately shy, and the marriage would be as good as consummated.

This little girl, however, was not shy. She sat out in the garden with Dr. Sadiq and tried every tactic of polite rejection, none of which seemed to work. Sadiq listened to me indulgently, and after many an hour of painful explanation on my part, would repeat his refrain: "Sara, I have fallen in love with you. Let me put this little ring upon your finger." After all logic had failed, I could not but help replying: "If that is the case, Dr. Sadiq, I would far rather marry you and be your second wife than marry one of your sons." Of course that was not true, but I think it drove the point home. Sadiq looked slightly alarmed—he had not really expected a counterproposal—but after that whole mess was over and he resumed his friendship with Pip, it is to Sadiq's credit that he welcomed me into his home without any reference to that fraught exchange. He even quite tenderly fed me pheasant for breakfast: perhaps he had fallen in love with me, after all. You are well remembered, Dr. Sadiq.

In some strange way, the idea of friendship seemed to take on an entropic course in Pakistan, so that the old relations Pip had with distinguished men such as Zahid Hussain and Amir Ali Fancy were substituted by alliances, with all the impermanence that an alliance suggests. There were such people as Majid Sahib and Mauj Sahib, but I do not wish to dwell upon Mr. Majid as editor of the *Nawai-e-Waqt* and Pip's overdetermined contact with that newspaper. We children called him Magic—I think with a degree of affection, although he was a very reticent man—and when Magic and Mauj came over for tea, which they did frequently, we raced off to Rahat Bakery to buy a plum cake and chicken patties for their delight. (Here allow me a digression. The British certainly made some culinary changes in the subcontinent, some for the worse, such as mango milk shakes, but others upon which the indigenous chefs did nothing but improve. I can honestly attest that I have never tasted a finer plum cake than that which came from Rahat Bakery, and as for chicken patties—well. That delicate, light puff pastry, filled—but not overfilled—with shredded *desi* chicken, seasoned—but not too much—with pepper, parsley, and a touch of garlic—well! Sometimes I wake in the night with a strange craving and can only whisper to myself, "Chicken patties, chicken patties." Who was it who said that food was the only desire that renews itself three times a day?)

Anyway, we were happy when Pip had the company of Magic and Mauj, the two M's, we would call them. And in some ways, they served us remarkably well. Pip needed distraction from his children, and when the M2's were ensconced in his room over tea, I do believe we could secrete a couple of our own friends into the house unnoticed. And then came the happy day when Pip told me, after his guests had gone, that the M2's planned to go to perform Hajj that year—together. He sighed, because that pilgrimage is certainly an acme in a good Muslim's career. "Why don't you go too, Pip?" I queried brightly. "So expensive," sighed Pip. "Well, next year it will be only more expensive, and you won't be going in the company of your good friends!" I urged. Pip looked up, piercingly. "Sara, you're right. I *will* go!" I beamed my approval on him and then raced off to take glad tidings to the rest of the household: "Pip is going for Hajj! Pip is going for Hajj!" Our joy, I'm afraid, had nothing to do with religion, but with the truth that three weeks without Pip's strict disciplinary habits constituted for us a glorious holiday. We were waiting for carnival, and as preparations were made and plans were sealed, I would only smirk demurely and look down as Pip repeated fondly to the family, "I owe this to Sara. It was Sara who urged me to go!"

And carnival it was. All the doors of 46 Gulberg 5, our home in Lahore, were cast open, while friends of all description trailed in with a heady sense of uninterrupted welcome. Even Khansama, our surly cook, seemed actually to smile and made no bones about producing batch after batch of his inimitable bread rolls ("raouls," he would call them, "raouls"), which we would devour in minutes and then would ask for more. Friends came and went, but our celebratory ways were certainly not defined as a freedom from Pip: in fact, they were a celebration of him. He was there in our mind's eye, swathed in white, behaving as an extraordinary pilgrim between Mecca and Medina. In our sleep we saw him move, solitary among at least three million other questers, surging around the Holy House of the Ka'aba. The pilgrims ebbed and flowed around the House in a space designed surely for hundreds as opposed to millions of bodies, at the heart of which—alone unmoving—lay the black stone of God.

"O Muhammad, *kamli-vala*," sing the Sufis. "O Muhammad, man with the blanket." It is a song of devotion and of intimacy, betokening a proud familiarity with a prophet who required nothing more of the world other than a blanket. And belief, of course. When Pip returned from his pilgrimage, we inevitably were at the airport to greet him. We half expected him to be shaved bald as sometime custom required of the pilgrim, but Pip was far too vain and his mane was still intact. For a man of good taste, he came back with some dubious gifts, such as some very shiny jewels for Tillat and one of those two-dimensional serrated photographs that present one image from a certain angle and a second from another. This picture, in full color, gave us "Mecca-Medina, Mecca-Medina, Mecca-Medina" until our eyes were forced to avert themselves from such holy sights. There was also the inevitable bottle of water from Ab-e-Zam-Zam, that sacred spring in the desert connected with a sweet story concerning a mother and a thirsty infant that I cannot quite remember. We solemnly partook of that holy water. To me, it tasted mustily stale and somehow lackluster.

So on Pip's return, the doors of our house in Gulberg 5 closed and locked again, although I sensed that others could be opening. Did I say it, or someone else, about the many mansions in my father's house? It began then, however, the slow unlocking, so that now I actually believe I can envisage it. Decades later, a door is being unlocked for Pip, allowing him to be received into the embrace of Muhammad the *kamli-vala*, his good and ultimate friend.

تم مرے پاس ہوتے ہو، گویا
جب کوئی دوسرا نہیں ہوتا
مومن

You are with me, as it were,
when no other can be there

— M Ō M I N

*T*here is a story, apocryphal no-dort, that Ghālib declared he would
have given his entire *divan*, his collection, to have written what Mōmin
wrote:

You are with me, as it were,
When no other can be there.

The sentiment is quite simple, its wrench lying only in the phrase
"as it were." That is, of course, another ineptitude of mine, but who can

provide me with a better translation of *goyah*? "So to speak," but in a single word? What is baffling about the *sher* (I increasingly hate the word "couplet," a most inaccurate approximation) is that its stark but gentle language conjures up a commonplace of love, of amorous discourse, but unsettles it by translating proximity into a metaphor. "Next to you, as it were; you close to me, so to speak; that no other can be acknowledged." All others are obliterated, except you who are also other.

Language. What a nuisance it is! I knew how pained Pip would be—almost as pained as was I—when I went like a blunderbuss through the delicacies of Urdu, which surely remained his most favored language. He was glad, I think, that I developed at least a nodding acquaintance with its poetry, but how he winced to hear me mismanage my sentences, again and again. I tried, and failed. Now I am convinced that my ability to lose language is almost greater than my propensity—one of my youth—to lose love, which was always in the foreground of discourse, as it were. "Love can make a foetus out of fear," someone has written, and my fear of losing whatever language I have remains persistent, germinating like a bead inside me. Remember such claims about words, how we forget them, how they forget us: "Then each precious dew drop falls / with my permission to be pearl."

In a way, my mother lived most of her life in translation. She never spoke Welsh, which her parents did; her French was merely academic; Urdu was one of those illusions that cast its shadow over her, but never long enough for her to possess it. As for Punjabi, it always struck us as a singularly male language: we even cringed slightly when Ifat taught herself to speak that red-blooded tongue with such gusto. The rest of us women remained monogamous, linguistically speaking, since monogamy is our wont in other matters, too. It makes a simplicity out of an existence already too prone to lascivious activities with complexity. And one of those complexities is surely the act of translation, which slips in and out of the most seemingly simple sentences, seizing them into new postures of articulation.

Cultures are certainly translated things: moving from one to another requires a discursive equilibrium hard to acquire, hard to retain. Once in New Haven, at one of those tediously familiar after-the-lecture receptions, a very well-meaning acquaintance beamed and said to me: "What cultural choices you must have to make each morning!" I consider myself relatively quick on the uptake, but this time I was lost. "Why each morning?" I inquired politely. "Oh, whether you wear Eastern clothes or Western clothes!" she beamed back. Now this did not provide room for a simple response. What was my nightdress, after all? Acultural? As an analogy, I would not presume to ask an acquaintance why she had chosen to wear black as opposed to gray stockings. "Look," I responded slowly, "I am a busy woman. I don't have time to lie in bed making cultural choices." I tried to explain that, as with everyone, it was a matter of pragmatics, such as the weather, or what was clean and readily available, and had no further symbolic significance at all. She just shook her head and smiled: I believe she thought I was being modest, whereas I think I was quite arrogant.

It must be the relative rudeness of American culture that allows its various inhabitants to say to me from time to time, "You are so exotic!" The phrase does not register as the compliment it is intended to be, because it seems to place my personage outside the ambit of a word for which I have increasing affection, which is "dignity." Now that is a quality that Mamma—translated though she was—possessed to a remarkable degree. Even those in Lahore who would smile at her Urdu could see it, could recognize how unusual she was in her understatement. When I in Lahore went out in a fit of misery for some careless sexual exploit, all Mamma said to me was, quietly, "You should not have, Sara. It is not dignified." If you could have felt a touch of my shame then, Pip, you would know that her response was far more arresting to me than yours could ever be. You would have ranted and raved, cited chapter, verse, and para of every ethical lingo, and no-dort would have locked me up in my bedroom for a while—for good, if you had your way. You really had a very strong urge to lock up your daughters, Pip, and look what good it did you.

Pip must have felt in his own way translated, not only through his uncanny knack of making families and friends disappear, but also through a contemplation of his brood. It would be hard to say that we are more Mamma's children than his, but surely we are closely aligned

to the habits of her sympathy. There was a certain form of melting ado-
ration that she received from us—this was true of her stepdaughter, Nuz,
as well—but with Pip our manner was slightly different, combining
amusement with admiration. Perhaps without our knowing it, we were
changing lingoes all the time, even within our selfsame language. I felt
quite startled when I read a touching little poem my niece Heba had
written for her mother. "Why can't one place be home?" she wrote, and
I wondered about the shifting sands that must occur when little sister,
rich and strange, transmutes into mother. There was a similar poem,
written for another mother, that seemed to embarrass you, Pip. Strange
thoughts of different times:

> "I dreamt that all last night it rained
> But I was deaf and neither could I see
> When I awoke my face was wet with tears."

I don't know why it made you fidget. Perhaps there was another
martial law in the offering, which is, on a civic level, yet a variant on
the mode of translation. Something, however, made you restless when
I read to you:

> "There was a shadow in the door
> When I moved out to seek the sun
> It drew me back into the moonlight of your ways."

What is the change of light but a form of movement, of becoming?
A Lahore twilight was around us, a quick and winning gesture toward
change, with the *motia* and *Rath ki Rani* cascading their perfumes toward
us. ("It's that damned *Rath ki Rani* [queen of the night] stinking at us
again," I said bitterly in C.B. College. But that's a different story.) You
sought something other than my words—maybe a newspaper always at
your hand—and did not deliberate much upon my recitation. I cannot
remember where Tillat was, or Irfan: it was simply Papa and me alone
on wicker chairs on the lawn, with Mamma elsewhere. I tried to tell Pip
what I had to read:

"All that I am once came from you,
From day to day, it burdens me,
The knowledge that our debts stretch overdue."

Pip did not really want to listen. Instead, he watched the fireflies gather in their charming fashion in the moist corners of the garden, never biting, never causing an itch, but merely casting out their intermittent gleam in a very hypnotic fashion. But still I persisted in my reading:

"Stretch over empty hours till I rebel
And promise eyes that see and lips that tell
I pledge my deepest dreams as rain for you."

"Do you think the gardener made a mistake with the roses?" Pip queried suddenly and irrelevantly, when I was done. I do believe that Tillat has a point, when she says Austin, with his habit of interruption, has certain alarming affinities with Pip. Of course I deny it vociferously, but must secretly acknowledge the fact. In the midst of flora and fauna—centuries ago—I had to admit that it was a painfully easy task for me to write a poem for Mamma, but that I have never, ever written a poem for you, Pip.

What a strange part poetry can play. I remember Mother Anunciata at Presentation Convent, who taught her group of wayward students to read *Macbeth*, line by line, word by word. (Years later, Tillat and her friend Shabana left me speechless when they, in preparation for a similar exam to the one I had taken, had memorized the entire play down to its last "what, ho!" And later still, how I doubly loved my admired friend Harold Bloom for writing, "The Macbeths are the only happily married couple in Shakespeare." Even more recently, Tillat disappointed me greatly by failing to complete the curse I was uttering in her direction: "Devil damn thee black," I told her, and was truly hurt when she did not chime in, "thou cream-faced loon!") But Mother Anunciata in Rawalpindi dragged us mercilessly through *Macbeth* and other Shakespearean items, and then had the grace to say to us, "*You* have great poets, too!" We did not quite understand her drift until she added, "Think of Gallop! Think of Ik-ball!" Oh yes, Ghālib and Iqbāl: translation is everywhere.

"Bless thee, Bottom, bless thee! Thou art translated," says a village yokel in A Midsummer Night's Dream when an exceedingly mischievious Oberon commands an equally mischievious Puck to anoint the admirable Bottom with an ass's head. The motive is to cause the estranged Titania—with the help of magic and love potions, of course—to become enamored of an ass, which she duly does. After much to-do, all ends happily ever after, but the translation of Bottom remains the most winsome, lightsome moment of the play. So it is possible for people as well as languages to translate: another way, I suppose, to describe the process of aging. A short while ago, I saw Tillat on our dock in Maine, watching me inch my way painfully down the ramp, moving precariously like a large sedated crab. Tillat had an anxious frown on her face; she looked at me as intently as though I were one of her children. I could tell that she was mourning something, the old Sara of yore, fleet of foot and sure of step. I felt sad to cause her distress, but even then could not help but smile at a fact she did not know. Standing there with a small anxious frown and slightly pursed lips, Tillat looked exactly like our mother.

I think we all must have looked the same during the long decades that brought you to your blindness, Pip. You were never completely blind and could always distinguish Tillat from me, Shahid from Irfan, even before we had uttered a word. But in the early years it made us wince to note the hesitation that had begun to intrude and obscure your firm tread. You recall, don't you, that in prior times—before your eyes turned treacherous—some doctor gently advised you to get more exercise. You got it into your head that a hundred brisk laps of the front lawn would constitute well over a mile, and for a while you kept to it quite diligently. At the twilight hour, Pip would stride purposefully into the garden to commence his laps. "You are napping; I am lapping!" he would say proudly, as we emerged one by one from our afternoon siestas. We were well aware of it, for the reason we had awakened was because Pip kept a stentorious count of his laps and his bellow of "thirty-six!" or "forty-two, forty-two!" would resound throughout the house. And so we ached when those dark days came along when Pip could not lap, could not walk—no, he could barely stand.

He never lost his voice, though, nor his laugh; they remained resonant forever. He would look up with undisguised delight when Shahid or I recounted some anecdote to him, a laugh already in his eyes before our sentences were done. And then, Pip always could surprise me. After my Ifat had been taken from us, I tried in a feebleminded fashion to make some poetry out of that loss. I must have sent Pip a couple of pieces, for the next time I was at home, he pulled out one of the shortest ones and said, "Sara, this is a beautiful poem. I am going to translate it into Urdu." To my knowledge he never did, but the very fact that he could express such a desire struck me as a high honor and a startled joy. I think I remember which one it was, Pip, so I am going to translate it for you: not from language to language, but from person to person, and on this score, you must concentrate. I am changing the gender in these lines to construct a palimpsest of sorts, so that it becomes a poem for you. Far be it from me (one of your favorite phrases) to eradicate Ifat from it, so you must read it as though her voice had been translated into mine, and that this is a poem she has written for you:

"They put the earth upon him, my first love,
    Heaped their instruments and drowned him in the ground!
    Put on him what you will of all things physical,
    Your stone upon his flesh, but lift
    The tyranny of your dear thoughts,
    And lift them, lest he feels the weight."

رقیبوں نے رپٹ لکھوائی ہے جا جا کے تھانے میں
کہ اکبر نام لیتا ہے خدا کا اِس زمانے میں
اکبر الہ آبادی

The pious keep going to report to the authorities:
That Akbar actually names God, in this very age!

— A K B A R   A L L A H A B A D I

*O*h, what a registry of complaints Pip kept reporting to his own authority! It did not matter if they had to do with his children, his wife,
his enemies, or his gardener. There was simply a register of ill-doing
that he would harvest and keep close to his heart. I often feel sympathy
for the hard-pressed telephone operators who used to be the victims of
his rage. Pip sat in bed surrounded by at least five different telephones:
when each one rang, methodically, periodically, he would utter a curse
into the mouthpiece, not too different from "God damn it! Son of a
bitch, son of a bitch!" (Austin's favorite refrain.) For the phones often

did not work, and certainly not when two were ringing at the same time. But Pip could not do without his telephones. With his lifelines set up, he could prop himself upright in his bed and roundly curse each innocent copy editor for failing to intuit what the next headline of the day should be. I feel sorry for his employees, erstwhile as they are, for who should be expected to be privy to Pip's outrageous energy, demanding attention when it surely was not deserved? Did he not know that implements, however efficient, were never well-enough equipped to say what he must say?

But the telephones that surrounded Pip in his latter years were like a nosegay, with him sitting beside them in bed like a veritable May queen. "It's the green one that's ringing, the green one!" he scowled and shouted, while his children would scurry to find the phone that was disturbing our tranquillity. Most calls would bring Pip peace, and we children were well accustomed to the salutations that would surround each numberless phone call. "*Mazaj-Sharif,*" he would ask, "Your elegant health," if his caller had not preempted him. If so, Pip would respond: "*Allah-ka Fazel,*" "By the grace of God," and I find myself using that phrase in the most inappropriate situations. But Pip's language was too large for the telephone: there are phrases that he used that have somehow infiltrated his children's language, so that we still say "lovely"—his apostrophe for Mamma—when we address our disparate beloveds, and we still say "God bless," as did he, when we conclude our secular conversations by Pip's métier, the phone.

And then there was also Pip's pen. He had a pen that had to be lovingly filled with exactly the right ink, then handed to him, after having been wiped with a special lint-free felt, so that he could resume his task of asking the country whither it was going. Doubtless (I am tired of saying "no-dort") he had a point to be made, albeit a somewhat repetitious one. But the gold-nibbed Parker and the Mont Blanc were not simply pens to us: they were icons, accessories to his personality. I think all his children were slightly saddened to see Pip give up his beloved pens and take up with tawdry instruments such as the one with which I am now writing. A BIC! Exact Tip Roller! Aside from the potential obscenity of this appellation, how can writing happen without a sense of a nib that knows how words may configure? But the pens went as his *gatha* (writing board) did, the way of all flesh. Why Z.A.S. should relinquish his pen I cannot imagine, for even he seemed to see it as an integral manifestation of his being. In my mind's cataracted eye I still can see the blur of him writing, sitting in his old armchair, pen in hand, *gatha* on knee, amidst a bevy of brightly colored telephones.

Aside from eyesight, Z.A.S., my father, has a certain uncanny connection with A.G., my spouse. Neither can be called materialistic, but both possess an inordinate fondness for things. (Accept the present tense from me, Pip, for the time being: consider it not oversight but as a token gift.) I think Z.A.S.—who had his own itineraries—would perfectly understand A.G.'s solemn desire to inventory all the items without which life would not be worth living. I drew up a catalogue for him once:

Number One: *Mermaid*, his yacht
Number Two: EBS, his company
Number Three: Tatty, dog of joy and humor
Number Four: Windwhistle Farm
Number Five: Last but not least, me, and I should be grateful for being on
    the list at all.

I know that Pip would have respected such priorities, which fitted with his sense of the scheme of things, so that it was indeed suitable for his daughter to be thus ranked. He ranked each of us several times, although there was a certain indiscriminate quality to his habit of forgetting which name belonged to the precise body he wished to summon. "Ifat-Tillat-Nuzhat-Sara!" he would bellow, even though there was only one of us that he required. Each of us would come running: if possible, we would still be running to his side today.

And then there was also the pipe. It was a brief episode in Pip's flirtation with tobacco, for he soon rejected it to return to his much-loved cigar. But while the pipe remained, he would hand it to one of us with a calm injunction, "Sara, clean my pipe." It was a more complicated task than I realized, separating bowl from stem and thrusting pipe cleaners down its orifices. We used to be fond of pipe cleaners, and in our childhood could twist them into all forms of ingenious and mythological animals. To use them for their actual purpose, however, was a thing apart. It gave me a new disgust for nicotine: for a committed smoker, I have a surprising disgust for nicotine. "Sara, clean my pipe." I was reminded of that injunction when, years later in Williamstown, Pip pronounced on the telephone, "Potenza, speak to my daughter."

Poor Mr. Potenza. He lived in Texas and Pip was in the States to purchase a fancy new printing press for his newspaper—it must have been the *Pakistan Times*—and Potenza had the ill luck of being a printing-press salesperson. He did indeed have a very heavy Texan accent, so Pip had not a clue of what he was saying when he described the little plane that would pick Pip up in Houston and fly him to the plant, where he could see any number of printing presses for his delight. So I spoke to Potenza on Pip's behalf and must admit his locutions were a trouble even for me. I was teaching at Williams in those days and so could not accompany Pip to Texas, where the press was duly viewed, examined, and bought. It was expensive, and I am not sure that it did the *Pakistan Times* much good, as the unions reminded its editor, but it indubitably made a valuable addendum to Pip's children's vocabulary. Henceforth, the word "potent" transmuted into "potenza," pronounced with a heavy Urdu accent. "Are you sure it will not be too potenza?" Tillat asked me, as I sliced for culinary pleasure green chili after green chili of the cayenne variety, which is such a neglected vegetable in the West. "Potenza is what potenza does" was my fine response.

Pip knew the value of objects. There was a time in Lahore when Irfan in his babyhood became obsessed with playing a monkey-man's role. This requires elucidation. The monkey-men were itinerants who went from house to house with their band of trained monkeys, and the latter performed for a certain fee any number of ingenious tricks. The monkey-man played on his *dug-duggi*, which also should be explained. A *dug-duggi* is a small drum, shaped like an hourglass, with tight leather skins on both ends and a couple of little pebbles affixed to leather thongs, so that when the monkey-man flexes his wrist, most marvelous music emanates from the *dug-duggi*. And he keeps up a running commentary: One of my favorites was when the man told his monkey, "Be a gentle*man*!

Be a gentle*man!*" And the monkey would go to the sack of implements, pull out a minuscule top hat, don it, clasp a baby walking stick in his paw (do monkeys have paws?), and strut along the driveway as though he were on the Strand. No wonder the monkey-men are so depleted, for the memory of the British ruling class is no longer available to the collective cultural imagination of Pakistan. They have gone, even from our remembrance.

In any case, our little Irfani, the youngest child of all, became totally absorbed with playing at being a monkey all winter long in the sunny afternoons when we sat outside in the Mayo Road house. That was fine by us, except that he required an adult to play the role of the monkey-man, so that one of us—and it was usually Pip—had to interrupt his conversation to wave an invisible drum and repeat the chant "*Bandar-vala aya!*" ("The monkey-man has come!") Irfan would perform his tricks and then hop solemnly up to each of us to collect his equally invisible fee. It was something of a distraction, and when Pip was for some reason in a store that sold artifacts, including a monkey-man drum, he bought it immediately for his son. Farni was so enchanted that he actually fell off the sofa, bruising his baby forehead into a painfully ugly lump. No ice, no compacts, could alleviate the pain of that beautiful little boy, and he went to sleep sobbing, but still clutching to his chest and chin the drum, the *dug-duggi* of his desire. Where are you today, Irfan.

"Potenza, speak to my daughter." At least he gave me warning, for one of Pip's most irritating habits was to hand the phone over to whomever was in his presence, pronouncing to me, "Sara, speak to X." Now in matters of telephonic conversation I still am monogamous, so it unnerves me to be told without warning, "Speak to X," no matter whom the X may be. Shahid has picked up Pip's manner, in quite an exasperating fashion. I thought I had not, until Mehreen rang me quite recently, and I simply handed the phone over to my sister saying, "Speak to Tillat." The only good part of this transaction was that Tillat understood I was not exaggerating when I said that Mehreen exudes an unwitting sexuality from her pores. "Her voice," my sister marveled, "it is like Bette Davis or Marlene Deitrich!" Those two have never met—my sister and Mehreen,

I mean—although I believe they will. I would like to implement that occasion.

Implements. I like it when Tillat bosses me, which she does frequently, about the color of lipsticks or the way my hair falls or what jewelry I should wear. "Sara, don't put on another necklace," she reproaches. "One alone looks so pretty!" I obey her slavishly and am glad she has not yet said, "Sara, why do you have two eyes? One would look so pretty!" for I know my obedience is of a kind that I would forthwith be gouging out an eye in order to receive her approval: "Sara, that looks so pretty!" We have a complicated medium of exchange, and—in terms of objects—much has to do with an amethyst. Here, I must pause. The stone entered our lives when Pip came back from Russia with a ring for Mamma, one that years later Tillat reproduced for me in Kuwait. I love the ring, which I have worn for decades, but my sister was most indignant when she saw it on my hand. "A dull stone! So dull! That cheat of a jeweler!" she declared, in a manner with which my siblings—willynilly—repeat and remind their audience of Pip. And so she procured for me another amethyst and dragged me off—sister like a little lamb—to a jeweler's in Ellsworth, Maine.

The stone setter was not there, so we whiled away some time, until Tillat began comparing her stone, her gift, to others that inhabited one of the jeweler's cases. Unfortunately, a little blurb attended those amethysts. There Tillat read: "In ancient times, the Greeks considered amethysts as a ward and a protection against intoxication. It was considered to be a safeguard against Bacchus." Oh dear, I thought, as Tillat read. "Sara!" she exclaimed as she perused this information. "No wonder your stone went dull! No wonder I bought you anther!" There I waited patiently, patiently, patiently, as Tillat waxed on. "I'm going to send off for a dozen more, grind them up, and put them in your drinking water!" Luckily—to date—this threat has not reached fruition. But I still stand there, at attention.

Perhaps language was our only implement, after all. What gave Shahid such ferocious power over Tillat but his ability to chant, incessantly, "Mushtabshera, *hamla tera*"? Here I must pause. Mushtabshera is not exactly a common name in Pakistan; by no means is it of the Tom,

Dick, and Harry variety. But little Tillat at her junior school did indeed have a friend called Mushtabshera. Part of me groaned inside me when Tillat in all innocence mentioned her friend's name to Shahid, and I had guessed well. "Mushtabshera?" repeated Shahid with surprised delight. "*Mushtabshera?*" He immediately began to concoct rhymes of epic dimensions to go with that somewhat epic name, and we all had to agree that the best he came up with was "Mushtabshera, *hamla tera!*" It rhymes, of course, and even scans well, and what it means is "Epic name, the attack is yours! Epic name, the attack is yours!" We gradually became accustomed to hearing that refrain throughout the house, whenever Shahid wished to make us rally round. The sad part is that Tillat would hear him, chuckle a little at first, and then out of sheer loyalty to her friend, burst into tears. She had already had enough of the teasing that reminded her she had no nose (she doesn't), or that her lips had been slivered away like an almond (not true). She did not need to bear the cross of a friend called Mushtabshera.

But Tillat got her revenge. I don't think that Pip had any idea of how Shahid lost his irony, his perpetual sarcasm, when he tried to teach his youngest two siblings sports. Luckily, I was excluded from this activity. For a while he taught them cricket with a proper cricket bat and a tennis ball; then he decided they were ready to graduate to the real ball itself. The ball, you know, is quite hard (Is it wood with red leather stitched all around it?), and Tillat did not look happy at its prospect. Shahid, commentating all the time, loped up to give an overarm bowl to Tillat. My sister looked steadily at that hard object, but the moment it came close to her vicinity, she flung down the bat, deserted her stumps, and ran off to the farthest point of the garden. This happened several times, and Shahid would be driven mad with rage. "Tillat," he said, "Tillat! What kind of sportsman are you?" "I'm not a sportsman," Tillat replied quite accurately, and wandered off calmly, making daisy chains. "You bastard," Shahid muttered under his breath. "And don't call me buster!" Tillat shrieked back, if it is possible to shriek with dignity.

Pip, of course, was too absorbed with his own instruments to pay any attention to the grief that accrued around a cricket ball. All he needed were his proofs and poor patient Dar Sahib—his secretary—scootering back and forth from home to office with revision after revision. Our evenings were quite fraught, therefore, with Shahid screaming at the children, me laboriously transcribing Pip's chiseled sentences, and Mamma keeping the peace. It is no wonder we needed respite and would drive out—outside Rawalpindi—to the startling peace of the Misriot Dam. It is a hidden secret of the city: everyone knows about the Rawal Dam and Rawal Lake, but few seem to know about Misriot. We went there once the evening promised respite from the heat, to stroll across those rocks—surely volcanic structures—and breathe in the soothing presence of the lake. Pip rarely accompanied us on these jaunts: it was lucky, for he was too impatient, and the pot-holed road that led us to the dam was not one he could endure. The lake itself was solitary, a body of water unto itself, and who knows how many ions of sustenance we imbibed from its spirit. On one occasion, trailing back over the rocks to the car, Tillat said, "Stop, Sara. Look." She pointed, and I saw two giant turtles with as many crevices as those in the rocks, sunning themselves, cooling themselves, as ancient as a moment of revelation, out of time.

And, Pip, do you remember how much you hated Shahid when he took us for a picnic up the Margalla Hills, the giant backdrop of Islamabad? It was in fact Major Naqvi's fault. He was a soft-spoken, genial bachelor who lived alone in the domiciles provided by the Rawalpindi Club. Major Naqvi could quite happily live in the club rooms, appreciate the kitchen's chips and club sandwiches, but occasionally he would mention, wistfully, "*mash ki Dal.*" Those are a particular kind of lentil, coaxed into exquisite flavor with garlic, onions, cumin, coriander—and everything else that brings tears of solitude to my eyes. Pip liked Major Naqvi, a distinguished, gentle human being, and so in a spirit of affection proposed that he should come on a picnic with us, in which the pièce de résistance would be *mash ki Dal.* Shahid enthusiastically volunteered to take us up to a spring in the Margalla mountains: some hours later, Major Naqvi planted himself next to the brooklet, panting, knees aquiver, and with no appetite at all for the *mash ki Dal* that we kept encouraging on him. Pip looked simply disgusted. "Why have you brought us here?" he addressed the chastened Shahid. "Do you really think we need to trudge five miles upward in order to eat *mash ki Dal?*

We could have eaten it at the club in half a jiffy!" Pip was never a believer in complete jiffies; they were either halves or quarters, or segments that you would not believe a jiffy could sustain. Nonetheless, he did everything in a half or best the sliver of a jiffy.

And Shahid ruined our lives and our toes once more, by taking us up to the peak of the Margalla Hills when our cousin Yasmin (Uncle Nasim's daughter) was visiting Rawalpindi. We cousins set off quite valiantly, and it was only after one long and hot hour that I realized I should not have put on the brand-new knickers that I sported. On a bed they looked quite sportive—floral, gay—but on the bottom they were an entirely different matter. They crept. They sought out indentations of the body that make walking quite an attitude of rumination. I would lag behind our jolly troupe, merely to pull out my knickers from where they did not belong, and my feet hurt badly, too, on my slow descent, for I had let the others in their gaiety go off far beyond me. As I went painstakingly down that mountain path—sometimes walking backward to ease my feet—I met an elderly hills man who watched me and then said compassionately, "*Soti le ke chal, mere lal.*" That means "Use a walking stick when you walk, my lovely." I could have wept when I heard that, Pip, because the man was so comforting, and I was in so much pain. His injunction was one I repeated to myself for years to come: he knew what instruments of any support were, and what they have to do with pity. I still say to myself, "*Soti le ke chal, mere lal,*" when I feel that all implements are abandoning me.

نہ چھیڑ اے نکہتِ بادِ بہاری ، راہ لگ اپنی
تجھے اٹکھیلیاں سوجھی ہیں، ہم بیزار بیٹھے ہیں
انشا

Don't trouble me, you perfumed wind, take to your road!
You have frivolity on your mind while I sit here in despair

—INSHA

It was after he turned sixty and turned religious, too, that Pip started to arise earlier than ever. I must admit that it has to be the best time in Lahore, a summer dawn when the air is almost buoyant before the onslaught of the heat descends. Pip would get up to say his prayers, go into the kitchen while everyone was still in bed, and make two cups of tea, one for himself and one for my Dadi, his mother. (Now, Dadi, don't get pettish. I know I have not mentioned you thus far in these threadbare sentences, but it is not neglect, I promise you. I contemplate the idea of you as though it were a distant thunderstorm or something more formidable: a Hurricane Dadi, in fact. To approach your subject would be to open such a can of worms that I would have sufficient bait to catch every finny thing in the Maine waters, and my few words would be swallowed, drowned. So don't be peeved. I am safer sticking to your son.) Pip in the kitchen is a peculiar thought, since it was not his customary haunt, as was the little ritual with which he took tea to my Dadi, for they had given up mutual speech several years ago. Still, they could have their tea in their separate rooms and then as though by clockwork could start chanting—no, singing—from their separate Qurans. I was still asleep but can wager a guess that their vocal chords were in slight competition: by the time I awoke, their Gregorian chant was reaching its summation, with a vociferous "Ameen!" (amen) rolling out from one side of the house and "Ameen!" (amen) from the other.

The weather in Lahore. It is a subject as unfailingly absorbing as weather in Maine, or anywhere else, for that matter. When Jinnah flew to London in pre-partition days, Pip was at the airport to meet him along with a host of reporters asking for a statement. "And what shall I talk about?" said Jinnah to Pip, looking at him affectionately. "The weather, sir," replied Pip, "the British always talk about the weather." Jinnah laughed, advanced to the microphone, and said in his elegant fashion, "I think I have brought the sunshine to London." (That man modest? No, Pip, come on, Pip, think again.) There is a photograph of that exchange: I do not own it, but devoutly wish that I did. Perhaps Tillat has it; perhaps Shahid, but not—alas—Irfan. They stand together with Pip looking radiantly up at his Leader, appearing so slender, appearing so glad. That is one thing to be said for you, Pip—there was no dearth of joyous moments in your life.

Lahore's weather. The summer was a time of brave endurance for us all, when even muslin weighed upon one's skin with the burden of a heavy wool. When Ifat and I shared a bedroom, we did not dream of lying on mattresses, those infernal reservoirs of heat: instead, we lay down on marble floors beneath the fan with a *mugga* (mug) of water beside both of us. We would sprinkle ourselves liberally with water several times a night, but during particularly oppressive hours, I would say: "Ifat?" "Yes?" "I am taking off my *battam*" (pajama bottom). "I am, too."

Some long seconds later, "Ifat?" "Yes?" "Let's take off our *taps*" (tops). "Good idea." So we girls lay there nude on a summer night, on marble floors in little pools of slippery water, with *muggas* being refilled almost on the half hour. I don't know what the men did in such moments of extremity. It was only Dadi who slept outside, alone beneath the stars.

The heat could make one gloomy. It took up so much of our concentration, allowing for nothing other than the refrain "Stave off the heat; stave off the heat." The dust storms were a peculiarly horrid phenomenon, particularly when the dust remained suspended in a windless air. Those murderous jets, waiting in Kuwait, know such dust today. "Storm away, and then go, dust!" I would implore, while the dust remained implacably inactive, coating our skin, our furniture, and even our teeth with its overpowering grit, its sandiness. And Lahore is not even next to the sea. But it pelleted us with grains that belonged to a different hemisphere, cloudy motions, while we would just stand there, frozen by the heat. Yet there were some saving graces to the summer, such as mango season, although I was never too much of a devotee of that potenza fruit. There were over a hundred varieties of them, in all shapes and sizes, all with fantastic names that I will not stop to catalogue. I did not relish them with the ardor that the rest of my culture did, but I must confess that in America when I am confronted with what this culture calls a mango, my lips curl with scorn. There is a hemispheric difference between them: these ones are generic, squat, thick-skinned. They are not even elegant enough to deserve individual names. "Come to Pakistan," I announce, "if you really want to eat a mango!"

And summer is of course *lassi* time. What a marvelous lunchtime drink that is, made of crystal water, yogurt, and salt, blended to perfection with some ice! Sometimes to the consternation of my husband, I make myself a large glass of *lassi* for breakfast, but it is not quite the same. For one thing, an electrified blender tends to neutralize the liquid, robbing it of the surprising consistency created by expert palms wielding a *riruk*. A *riruk* is a wooden instrument, with a stem and then some surprising wooden fins that are rotated in the yogurt and water to produce a beverage unchallenged in its succor and delight. I should have asked Tillat to bring me a *riruk* when she was last in Pakistan.

Pip thought London was a very damp and drizzly town, and he announced the fact as though he were the first person to notice it. He would recount this splendid truth as a prevailing feature of his first sojourn in London, the other prevailing feature being my mother. "And you know," said Pip with a little smile, "in those days, I didn't even think she was pretty!" I can accept that as a tiny idiosyncrasy—maybe all Europeans looked the same to him, as we Orientals all look alike to the rest of the world—but it riled his son considerably. "What nonsense!" says Shahid in his most prickly fashion. "In those days she was gorgeous, absolutely gorgeous!" I agree, and then, "she always was," he adds. It gives me pleasure to think of Mamma in London during those days: she was heartsore for her brother Hugh, then a prisoner of war in a German camp, but by all accounts was so perky, so alive. Her mother, my nana, would tell us proudly: "And when Churchill came to the Admiralty, he would say, 'Where is my little Welsh girl?' and then beam when she appeared." That's not really a surprise, Pip, for in those days she was so unwittingly your lovely and with a radiance too young for common sense. She always was, as Shahid will add.

It was a winter in Lahore when Ifat looked at Tillat to say, "As you grow older, I will only love you more and more!" Tillat was touched, flattered, and asked her softly, "Why?" "Because then you will look even more like Mamma than you do now," Ifat declared with ceremony. I suppose that is a double-edged compliment, for to be told you will be loved passionately for someone you are not is a somewhat peculiar place to be. It is not Tillat's fault, for even she acknowledges that she can be engaged in something as pedestrian as washing her face and when she looks up at the mirror, she sees Mamma gazing back at her. The resemblance is uncanny, but I believe it has less to do with feature than with habit, a cast of expression, a sudden turn of the head. Pip, in his walking and seeing days, has come into his bedroom to see Tillat languishing on a bed or a chair. He has stood there arrested. He does not see his daughter but his wife.

The winters in Lahore have changed, they tell me, which is saddening, because when that sky cast off its petrified heat to become blue again, what relaxation entered each tendon and muscle of our bodies! It became a sky of startling blue, and our afternoons were long, luxurious. Sitting out in the garden sunlight, there were peanuts, cashews, pistachios at hand for our pleasure, as well as pine nuts—not the stubby, stale things that America offers you, but kernels slender, delicate, and fresh. And part of the satisfaction of those nuts was the shelling of them: they came heated out to us in straw bowls, and we would shell them, each unto ourselves, while stories and anecdotes floated between us. Pop went the peanut, pop went the pine nut, as a very satisfactory punctuation mark to our tales and our laughters. In Paki theatrical lingo, laughter always occurred in the plural, as though each clap were a countable thing. And on the subject of American offerings, doesn't a certain statesman with close-set, shifting eyes look remarkably like a weasel?

But now, I am told, the pollution over Lahore is so great that they never hope to see such a brilliant blue again, and face instead a sky that is always dim and receded. I hope it is just a fashion. There was a time in the last ten years when kidnapping became a fashion in Lahore, and Karachi, too, for that matter. The chic thing to do was to own a Pajero SUV, have a Kalashnikov machine gun in the backseat, and trot out to kidnap people, much as though one were setting out for a matinee film or an early evening play. The various industrialists, bureaucrats, would-be politicians, and their children would either show up after the ransom was paid, or they would not. I am glad to say that this fashion seems to have become a bore in recent years. That is heartening. Perhaps after the torture that accompanies those colorful adventures—both in prison, both in the hands of the kidnappers—kidnapped and kidnappers alike have decided to turn to the environment instead and give back Lahore its limpid winter skies. It would be pleasant.

It is hard to describe the monsoon rains and the way they would come down at right angles in a proper and soul-refreshing sheet of rain. America still troubles me when its storms approach and it seems a perfect theatrical setting for a real storm. It dies, however, after a parsimonious five minutes of rain, and we are left quite parched. Even Pip enjoyed the rains. He would emerge from his writing in his favorite summer garb, swimming trunks—not in use since our stint by the Karachi beaches but an ideal garb for a worn armchair, in which to sit, writing sentences. Something of that attire must have rubbed off on to the articles themselves, for when they were published in newspapers that he did not edit, they were almost invariably accompanied by the disclaimer "Views expressed in this column do not necessarily express those of the whatever *Times*." Pip called that small italicized caveat his "bikini," and on the few occasions it did not appear, would exclaim, "Where is my bikini? To leave me standing naked just like that?" The monsoons would bring Pip out in great glee: he burst running into the rain, laughing heartily, and thrashed about in that steady and purifying liquid as though he were a butterfly. A big one, of course, but still a butterfly. We children pranced around him—also in swimming suits—and I realized when I was ten years old: "Oh! Pip is just a child."

The first monsoon rains would call for festive meals, such as mangoes with *lassi* and *dal-bhari roti*, which is unleavened bread, flattened out into tortilla-shaped rounds. *Dal* is lovingly spread upon the *roti*, a second *roti* is clapped on top, and then the structure is fried with care in clarified butter. When someone told me that I was essentially describing a sandwich, I took affront. "Sandwich" is far too crude a word to apply to that miraculous bread, in itself a total meal. To partake of it was joyful, but a monsoon evening would also bring out the *parvana*s in full force. *Parvana*s: how shall I represent them? They are insects. Despite their prominent role in amorous Urdu poetry, they remain insects with wings that flock toward any available light, be it a lamp or a lightbulb, and I have seen them translated as moths in England—the desire of the moth for the lamp is certainly quite pleasing and romantic—but they're not moths. They are much smaller, worms with wings. And the trouble is that they discard their wings overnight, once the lights are put out, so you wake in the morning to find *parvana* wings scattered all over the floor, crisping beneath your feet. I asked my mother where the worms got to, but she didn't know. Perhaps they wiggled into the garden and sprouted fresh wings when the lights came on. In any event, the experience is not nice. I do not know what Urdu poets were thinking of when they hit upon the *parvana*/lamp metaphor as one of their favorite figures for desire. I am fond of desire myself, but not of worms with wings.

Once, in Islamabad, beloved Eqbal Ahmad was walking me back from a conference room to my rest house when I noticed that the evening air was filled not with *parvana*s but with bats. The eerie thing about bats is that they are so silent: you look up and think you see a cloud until you realize, no, this is the motion of a living thing, moving with intent. Some old folktale had told us that bats like to nest in women's hair, with the ultimate aim of sleeping in their ears. Not a pleasant thought, but luckily the walk was short and I was distracted by Eqbal, who was talking gently about Fanon, with whom he worked in Algeria. "Poor Ifrantz!" Eqbal sighed. "He died so young!" Ifrantz was of course Frantz: there is a certain Urdu spoken in Lucknow that insists on adding a vowel before an opening consonant, so that Frantz has to be Ifrantz, school has to be ischool.

The conference we were attending had to do with "Pakistan and Sustainable Development"—I am still not certain how to gloss that title. It gave all of its participants, however, a happy time, and I was glad to be with Ayesha Jalal, my distinguished historian friend who has written about Jinnah. She is also doubly distinguished by the fact that she invariably clads her birdlike body in the most pristine cottons and muslins, perfectly starched, and also walks at a pace that rivals Achilles: Ayesha/Achilles, fleet of foot. When she was chairing a sustainable development panel that had to do with feminism, one of the more conservative members of the group made the mistake of saying: "Why don't you ladies simply provide us with a list of do's and don't's?" It loses its charm without a very heavy Urdu accent. Ayesha drew up her dignity, which is considerable, and uttered scathingly: " 'Do's and don't's'? Then don't! Then don't! Then don't!"

Eqbal was completely enchanted by such exchanges, which became quite vociferous. He would smile gently and look up, casting his eyes to opposite corners of the ceiling. Later, during our coffee break, he asked me, "Sara, what are your do's and don't's? How remiss of you not to tell me how to sift your do's and don't's!" Much later, when Eqbal was to retire from Hamshire College, I was asked to speak at a farewell conference held in his honor. He was about to return to Islamabad to press on with his harebrained, quixotic scheme of opening a proper university in the country's capital. It would be named Khaldunia, after the great Arab scholar. Now, of course, the project has disbanded and its trustees dispersed. At Hamshire College, however, when I was one of the speakers, Eqbal looked most amused when I titled my talk "In Praise of Hypochondria." It was designed as an ironic trope, for I did call Eqbal a hypochondriac who took care of the manifold commitments of his life with such engagement, and such care. How was I to know that shortly after Pip's death, Eqbal would also wither with diseases unrelated to hypochondria? It was my dear friend Agha Shahid Ali who gave me the news: he called to say, "Eqbal has died," and we both burst into uncontrollable tears.* There is a strange intimacy to the telephone. It would only be spring in Pakistan—season of berries, *falsa*s and *jaman*s, choicest berries both—when Eqbal was put into the ground. I find myself adding to the catalogue of Ifrantz, saying, "Poor beloved Eqbal!" And then sighing, "He died so young!"

*And you, Agha Shahid Ali, to follow with your own leavetaking! Could you not have waited until another day?

ہم ہیں مشتاق اور وہ بیزار
یا الٰہی یہ ماجرا کیا ہے؟
غالب

We are the lover, they the impatiently disdaining:
Dear God! What kind of business is this, anyway?

— GHĀLIB

I cannot remember the time when Pip regarded all of his children in equal good favor. As I have mentioned, there were six of us, and never when we congregated around a luncheon table was Pip on speaking terms with all of us at the same time. Dadi at the foot of the table was always incognito, and I suspect rather enjoyed her status as persona non grata, which she played to the hilt. Pip was inevitably at the head of the table, Mamma to his right, while we children scrambled to find places as far away from Pip as possible. That was achievable, but then we still had to face the *phulka* trauma, lunch after lunch. *Phulka*s are freshly cooked *rotis*, light and full of steam, that the cook would make once we were at the table and the bearer would carry in, one by one. They would be deposited in a breadbasket next to Pip's place setting, and he was almost Christlike when he tore them in two and passed them down to his long line of children. There were obvious problems, however, when one of us was in Coventry, which was always. He did not deign to hand the disfavored any bread, which in a way was quite a relief, since lunch was much too big a meal anyway. Once, when I had the misfortune of sitting next to Pip and alongside Ifat, who was in disfavor, Pip kept piling my side plate with *roti* after *roti*. I did not dare know what to do until he snarled at me, "You selfish girl! Can't you pass on some bread to your *sister*?" I did so with relief, and as she and I exchanged glances of recognition, I knew this steaming piece of bread betokened a ceremony through which Ifat could pass from disfavor into favor.

It wouldn't last for long. And in the interim we had to endure the lunch of the bouncing *boti*. It tires me to explain what exactly that lunch may be. Consider a curry, made with mutton, into which a vegetable is also thrown. Think of it as a stew, if you will, but one highly spiced and delicately decorated with sautéed coriander and parsley. The meat in that *salan* is hard to describe: I would avoid it, sticking to the vegetables alone. (Years later, it made Shahida exclaim, "Look at Sara! She eats just like a Hindu!" I do not think the term was one of endearment in her lexicon.) In any case, the lunchtime *gol boti*, as they were called, happened to be rounded fragments of a meatiness that were considered most prized. "Oh, a *gol boti*, Zia!" exclaimed my mother. "You have it!" She bounced the *boti* at my father's plate. "No, you have it!" and Pip would bounce it back again. "No, you have it!" and off went the bouncing *boti*. It was as though two turtledoves were in dalliance, positively playing badminton with that *boti*. They accompanied it with loving smiles, our parents; the *boti* kept on bouncing, while their children just stared down at their plates, mashing veggies into smaller and smaller slivers.

When Ifat was in disfavor, it usually had to do with the man who was shortly to be her husband, a person on whom I do not wish to dwell. But with the rest of us, Pip's motives were far less easily defined. Shahid would be put in Coventry because his two schoolteachers had taken to dropping by our house on holiday afternoons: hardly a crime, you'd think, but it grated on Pip's nerves to no small degree. I did not wish to be Shahid when, on one winter afternoon, Pip returned from his office for lunch only to find the dining room occupied by Shahid's teachers and friends. Pip would not join them. He flounced out to the garden in high dudgeon, leaving strict instructions with the bearer to let us know the moment Shahid's guests had finished eating, so that he could have his lunch and return to work. The lunch lasted longer than it should have, to Pip's increasing impatience. I certainly did not wish to be poor Karam Dad, the bearer, when he came out to announce that Shahid and his friends had ended their repast, and then was forced to add: "How would you like your eggs cooked, sir?" "Eggs?" shouted Pip. "*Eggs*?" You see, the chicken curry had been polished off, as had been the rice, the lentils, and the veggies. I thought a luncheon omelet was a fine idea, but it put Pip into a fuming rage, and he wouldn't speak to Shahid for weeks on end.

Poor Mamma. She did her best to protect us from Pip's disfavor, and so would keep secret her routine visits to Father Byrne at St. Mary's, Shahid's school, or to Mother Baptist at Presentation Convent, my school, while we were still in Rawalpindi. (Tillat was also at the convent, but she was too small to be considered the epitome of misrule.) It seems we were always under threat of expulsion, and two incidents in the convent remain the most memorable to me. The first was when I persuaded two of my classmates to enter the bishop's garden—a territory strictly out-of-bounds—knock upon his door, and ask to be converted to Catholicism. Our story was as follows: we were three half-sisters, for our father had married three times, first to a Hindu, then to a Muslim, and lastly to a Lutheran missionary. Our beliefs were consequently in confusion, and we sought the solace of the church instead. The bishop looked perplexed: "Did your father marry these ladies simultaneously?" he asked. We girls did look remarkably close in age, and there was not a lot of family resemblance between us. But he heard us out politely, advised us to consult our father and multiple mothers, and to stop in the chapel on our way out for a moment of quietude and prayer. It was in the chapel, while we were shrieking with laughter, that Mother Baptist caught us. "You!" she whipped round at me. "You are the ringleader!" Did I have the mark of ringleader printed on my brow to be thus constantly singled out? The trouble is, she was usually right. "Honestly, Sara," Mamma mourned as I stood outside the principal's office in expulsion posture, "sometimes you go too far."

The second incident was during the month of Muharram, the opening month of the Islamic calendar. It has nothing of the chirpiness of a new year, really, since it also commemorates the tragedy of Karbala and the slaughter of Muhammad's relatives, an event that will make every Muslim sorrow. Today, the American news is full of "Ker-Bālla," as it is called: a spot emptied of history, a mere dot on the road map to Baghdad. And our class decided—there were only ten of us to a class—that we would lock up our book bags (tacchy-cases, they were called, as in attaché). We would then cover our heads, look mournful, and refuse to talk about anything but religion. Our Urdu teacher, a Mrs. Mustafa, was quite pious herself and totally approved of our piety: she lectured us for a good hour on the sad happenings of Karbala. The geography teacher, however, was not so amenable, and the biology teacher not at all. Miss Riaz declared to us, quite taken aback, that she knew nothing about religion, did not want to talk to us about religion, but wanted to teach us about cacti instead. We students feigned horror at such blasphemy, touched our ears to ward off evil, and solemnly trooped out of the classroom in single file, our heads duly covered with veils. "Come back!" shouted Miss Riaz. "Come back, come back!" We made a solemn progress down the corridor until we met my nemesis, Mother Baptist, habit aflying, bearing down on us with rage. And so I was back outside the principal's office until Mamma was summoned to plead for me. "Honestly," she said on our way home, "honestly, Sara, honestly."

There were some disfavors, however, from which she could not protect us. Ifat's runaway marriage was one, although the less said about that, the better. And Mamma could hardly intervene in the days when we lived in Rawalpindi and Shahid was sent to Aitchison College in Lahore. It was midterm; Pip was at home writing, when suddenly out of the blue Shahid arrived. Pip—always delighted to see his firstborn son—exclaimed, "Shahid!" and was quite ready to kill the fatted calf forthwith. But my brother was slightly uneasy. "I have brought a teacher with me," he ruefully explained. It transpired that while Shahid was in the Aitchison infirmary for some minor ailment, his mail was routinely opened by the matron, who was horrified to find that it contained some remarkably libelous and obscene lyrics about his various teachers, both in Rawalpindi and Lahore. They were coauthored by Shahid and his friends. She took them to the principal, Abdul Ali—a feudal gentleman if ever there was one—and Shahid was summarily expelled. Pip took up Shahid's case most vigorously, but Abdul Ali was not to be budged. It did not help matters much when I came into the drawing room one evening to hear Pip on the telephone, calling Abdul Ali a bull and a pig. The gentleman immediately challenged Pip to a duel, which he promptly accepted: a foolish thing to do, since the only weapon he had been known to wield was his tongue. Luckily the encounter never took place, and a chastened Shahid returned to complete high school in Rawalpindi, at St. Mary's, under the benevolent tutelage of Father Byrne. Pip never did say much about the porno poems of Shahid's that Abdul Ali had made him read: I have a feeling that he secretly admired them, porno though they were, for their wit and éclat. "My son is a writer, after all," he must have thought to himself with satisfaction.

So Shahid eventually went off to Cambridge to read law, along with the burden of Pip's designed-to-be-disappointed expectations. It wasn't Shahid's fault: he was too intelligent for that venerable institution, too innately prone to breaking rules. He would take on the strangest summer jobs, once selling ice cream in the London theater district and standing stock-still each time the actress sang "Bring in the Clowns," with tears pouring down his face at the chords of that admittedly moving song. Once he sold kebabs at a *Kebabchi* whose owner was an admirer of my father's, and soon came to be an admirer of Shahid's, too. "Shahid, my son," he would say with the greatest respect. "You should be a Punjabi film actor! With that voice, that face! I'll lay money on it that—if you put on some weight—within a season you would become a heartthrob star!" The *Kebabchi* notwithstanding, Shahid did put on weight, but to the best of my knowledge never became a Punjabi heartthrob film star. I rather regret it. I would have liked to see him bearing his chest, beating it, prancing around an extremely voluptuous actress, and conferring the impressiveness of his voice on an audience rather than on me.

And Tillat, in the middle of these traumas, what unnecessary rebukes she had to sustain! As the youngest daughter, I believe she was given some respite, but not on tiny issues, matters you should not have noticed, Pip. But you did. There was a time when she returned from Karachi after a fortnight with her friend Shabana wearing a denim pantsuit that would put Hillary Clinton to shame. Pip looked at her with a curved-lipped sneer: "And who do *you* think you're becoming, Tillat?" It brought her close to tears, and I felt it incumbent upon myself to declare, "But she looks very, very nice!" On the terrible day, which was close to the time of my departure for the United States, Tillat had—quite insequentially—put curlers in her hair and sat around the dining table with her head bound up in a silk kerchief. "If *you* think this is a good idea," Pip snarled, "you are wrong!" I would have tried to intervene, but it was not necessary. Dadi, from the opposite end of the table, looked up with considerable pleasure. "Aha," she said, "aha! Tillat has chosen to wear a turban! Aha!" We had to be silenced, no words allowed, when Dadi transmitted her pleasure to Tillat, and my father simply turned his head in a gesture of pure denigration. My Tillat sobbed later, over the ironing board, "At least he could have been kinder to you, on your last birthday at home!" "No," I told her, "no."

No. She was stronger than I was and could take sidelong recrimination more quietly than her sister could. Over one lunch, Pip looked up with his lips curling in disgust. He leveled his bushy brows at my sister. Tillat had plucked her eyebrows, as women are wont to do, but she was not allowed to forget that perfectly ordinary female activity. "Tillat!" said Pip, abhorrence exuding from his pores. "What have you done to your eyebrows?" That may have been after a *boti*-bouncing episode, so that a smile quite left his stern eyes. Around that overdetermined dining table, he would look at her with ultimate disgust, to add: "Look at Sara! How beautiful her eyebrows are! Not a single disfigurement of nature!" Since I had trotted off to have my eyebrows pruned that very week, I simply stared down at my meal and blushed modestly. Tillat

was about to make one of her "jolly well!" remarks, but she endured
the reprimand and only looked at me with understandable hatred. My
father then quoted poetry of a ludicrous extravagance about what bows
eyebrows are, what scimitars eyelashes are, so that our very faces were
transmuted to a battlefield. We looked down at our plates and specu-
lated whether our jawlines could be frontlines, or a twentieth-century
trench, the clefts in our chins. It would be fair enough, Pip, if you had
cast your sarcastic barbs in our direction and then left us, with the force
and strength of a bumblebee. But you didn't. You tended to chide us
before we should be chidden. And please realize, out of love for you,
Pip, we were busy inventing reasons for which you could keep chiding us.

I don't know which was worse for my brothers, the tenacious concentration Pip inflicted on Shahid or the benign neglect he adminis-
tered to Irfan. We were all at fault in leaving Irfan to his own devices,
although Ifat tried, while she was alive, to provide him with an alter-
native home; Nuz did so in Karachi, too; and he lived three years with
Shahid in London. I am sorry that he has never visited me in America,
an absence that could perhaps be remedied. We all have to remind ourselves that Irfani was the only one present when Pip came home with
his blushing daughter, Shahida, at his side. For one missing his mother
and his sister, that must have been a trauma. Irfan was working in the
advertising department of the *Pakistan Times* in those days and was quite
successful at it. In a moment of mutiny, however, the union members
of the newspaper challenged Pip about his appointment, citing someone from their clan as a substitute. How proud I felt of Pip when, rather
than defending himself by citing a list of Farni's many talents, he replied
with slow dignity, "He is my son. Would you rather I let him go to the
dogs?" You didn't, Pip. And today when I see Irfan working so hard in
Birmingham, with Attiya and their three children, there is something
dignified even in the air of his fatigue, and I know to say, "Yes, Pip, he
is your son."

In earlier times, however, when we were all at home, it soon became
clear to me that the only reason for my not being in more frequent disfavor was because I was too useful. Pip was politic enough to know that

he needed me to copy out his articles, to proofread, to care for Mamma, to cope with the cook. And I was politic enough to know my uses and to stretch like an elastic band the boundaries between favor and disfavor. The band would snap, of course, and sometimes on the most incomprehensible occasions. When I was invited to act in the Caravan Theater, a touring company, I was only given Pip's permission if I adopted a stage name, Saira Ahmad, and thus did not sully either Sara or Suleri. (I was twenty-one at the time. Why on earth did I need permission? Curious to contemplate today, but I most certainly did.) That arrangement was fine by me, because I liked to act at any cost, so Pip's reaction came as quite a surprise to me when—some months later—I wrote a play under the pseudonym of Saira Ahmad. That was only under the wise advice of Perin Cooper, my drama teacher at Kinnaird: the play was for a competition, and one of the judges was a columnist called Zeno, who was an archenemy of Pip's. In fact, they could not do without one another, for when news was low, they could always use their columns as a jousting ground: Zeno would send poisoned darts at Pip, and Pip would send them back to Zeno. In any case, Perin sensibly suggested that the name Suleri would not endear me to the adjudicators, and she was right. When I returned chirpily to announce to the family that my play had won an award, my father met me with one of his oft-repeated and memorable phrases—"Get out of my sight."

"It's really quite simple," Mamma explained to me incongruously later on in the evening. "He's just hurt that you would sell your birthright for a mess of pottage, for an award." I didn't even bother to mention that Pip's hurt feelings bore an uncanny resemblance to revulsion and rage, but tried to remind her that he was the one who made me change my name when it suited his purposes. "He *made* me do it, Mamma!" "I know, darling, I know," said my mother as though that was sufficient clarity. So for a while I was the one at whose sight Pip would dramatically avert his gaze, his lips curled in pronounced disgust. We children rallied round each other at such moments, and Tillat comfortingly reminded me that it sometimes was easier to be in Coventry than out of it. "Tillat!" Pip barked. "Take this article to your sister and tell her to copy it out." The fact remains that it was not sufficient for our persons to be put into Coventry: our very names became pariahs, anathemas not to be pronounced.

I was soon forgiven, but a curious feature of Pip's favor is that it never came accompanied by a definitive statement: there were tiny signals, little gestures beamed in our direction that we were meant to divine and interpret. We would leave for our schools or colleges as wayward black lambs and return to find that, mystifyingly, somehow during the day we had been translated into creatures as white as driven snow. "Tillat, come and sit next to me," Pip would roar genially. "Let me look at your no-nose, no-lips, your beautiful eyes and eyebrows!" A startled Tillat approached. "Now, Sara," he turned to me reproachingly, "why do you do such terrible things to your eyebrows? Look at what lovely eyebrows Tillat has!" We were left speechless, hardly able to follow the logic that put the spirit of our acceptability into our brows. But Pip was more wily than such rapid shifts of allegiance would suggest. "It's being humorous that keeps me going," he chuckled, disarmingly.

When I wrote poems, I always showed them to Mamma, never to Pip, in those days while I was still at home. I showed them to my siblings, too, who would always sigh with patience when I pulled out the bottom drawer of Mamma's lovely desk to present them with my latest scribbles. (That desk, what a strange history it has! In Wales my grandfather took his daughter to Vivyan Holland's estate, divine Oscar Wilde's son, when it was being dismantled. Choose a tree, he told her, which she did, and it was later transformed into a charming desk. We loved it passionately, both for her and for itself. She in her kindness declared it would always belong to the oldest daughter in the house. Where is that desk today, I wonder.) Anyway, my mother loved to see my writing, and I showed it to her as a secret gift. Once, however, she must have left a poem lying around, for when I came downstairs I heard to my horror Pip's Urdu accent repeating to itself:

"Voice of daisy, come to me,
  Take me to the holy tree,
  And in the shade of passion spent
  Sing solo of abandonment."

I think Pip was a trifle disturbed. " 'Passion spent'?" I heard him mutter, " 'Abandonment'?" So I stood outside his door and prayed he would read no more, but that was a vain belief:

> "Give me such beauty that I may
> Lie satiated night and day
> While sunlit specks of ashes float
> In leisure to your velvet throat.

" *'Satiated'*?" was Pip's commentary. " 'Specks of ashes'? What ashes? Does Sara smoke?" Recall that he was talking to himself. " 'Velvet throat'? *Whose*?" I wondered how much I could draw on theories of poetic license and realized immediately that it was not worth a try. Pip continued:

> "And flail of time, at last at rest,
> Goes bowing to the frightened quest,
> Who swells, who swells, oh glory be!
> With roots around the passion tree."

I was expecting an immediate sojourn of disfavor, particularly when I heard Pip repeat with some alarm, " 'Swells'? 'The passion tree'?" but luckily I was wrong. He never mentioned the poem to me, silly as it was, and we continued to be on the best of terms. Yet he was not without his barbs: he began to regard me with some dubiety and a new respect. When we were sitting out in the garden of an evening and the phone rang inside his room, he would say, "Run and get it, Sara! Run, for all you know, it may be the Voice of Daisy!" And then he would chortle, so pleased as he always was at his own jokes.

But, Pip, you would always laugh at ours. I still recall the countless times you repeated a tale of mine that I do not remember. We were in some European hotel, and for some reason the children were to be taken down to the formal dining room: perhaps a nanny service, along with room service, could not be procured for us. Pip lectured the three of us most severely—for there was only Ifat, Shahid, and I in those days—to say we were to come down to the dining room with our parents and be on our best behavior, if not . . . if not . . . he left his fearsome threat unuttered. So the five of us went down, doubtless a charming family, except when I looked up in the middle of the soup course and said sweetly, "Papa, I am going to be naughty in a minute." Oh, Pip, how you roared with laughter as you recounted and recounted that story! How could that tiny slip of a thing, your youngest child, put you into such a cold sweat of fear? I know now, however, how to amuse you if ever we meet in celestial realms: I'll say, "I'm going to be naughty in a minute," and then shall be in your favor, Pip, forever, quite forever.

پاک سر زمین شاد باد!
قومی ترانہ

Long live, you purest land!

— PAKISTANI NATIONAL ANTHEM

Pakistan: i.e., land of the pure, or the pure land itself; taken from either perspective, it is a great misnomer. Even my friend Marina would say, "No, no, no." (She has a wonderful emphasis to her voice and almost like Lear can never say "never" once, but instead: "Never, never, never, never, never." She will also say, my dear Marina, that she has been "cooking, cooking, cooking"; that she is tired of wearing "tents, tents, tents.") Pakistan has little to do with purity, as we all know. There is hardly any point in talking about the traffic, the sewers, the pollution. Nor do I want to linger too long on the governments or the constitutions that unfurl periodically as though they were annual plants. Zinnias, maybe.

104

Perhaps it is fitting, for a country so largely agricultural. But if you keep on nuclearizing bombs, importing guns and heroin and all their sweet refinements, where will you be, Pakistan?

I blame Zulu for this. We will be in strong disagreement, Pip, on such a subject, for you were quite chummy with that maniacal general. (He was general number three, wasn't he, to head the nation? Number one, Ayub; number two, Yahya; number three, Zulu. And now we are on number four. O Pakistan.) When Zulu responded to the Soviet invasion of Afghanistan with such rigor, he was quite a hero in the West. In a country already unable to deal with its own houseless, hungry populace, Zulu in his magnanimity allowed some three million–odd refugees into the northwest province of Pakistan, and they arrived equipped. The families and tribes must have journeyed through the Khyber Pass— the same unforgettable route that Alexander took a few centuries ago, yet at least he came with nothing other than an army that indubitably did litter the province with Grecian blue eyes—but the Afghans arrived with guns, drugs, and all the insidious trade those items imply. Not for a moment do I wish to suggest that Pakistan was innocent of such trade before the overtaking of Afghanistan: not at all, I only know of the miserable pressures it added to the nation's cities and to its fragile borders.

And on this score, I must give Zulu credit for one lasting comment. When Carter promised the Paki government a billion or so dollars of U.S. aid to assist the refugee situation, Zulu simply looked up, flashed his white-toothed smile, and told the reporters, "That is peanuts!" I think America and its press were somewhat offended by this comment, but surely we must admit it is rather amusing. As comic as were the circumstances of how Zulu got blown up over Bahawalpur. Some wag has it that the bomb was secreted in a case of mangoes, labeled "Man-go." Others insist that the accident only happened in late summer because the assassins could not bear to part with the best of the crop until the mango season was past its prime. We shall never know.

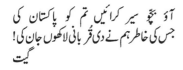

آؤ بچّو سیر کرائیں تم کو پاکستان کی
جس کی خاطر ہم نے دی قربانی لاکھوں جان کی!
گیت

Come, children, let us take a little tour of Pakistan!
For whose sake we have lost so many lives, so much *jan!*

That's quite a fine translation, even if I say so myself. But isn't it a peculiar song to teach to young children, who are constantly reminded of the blood upon which this nation was inexorably built? Songs, however, we were taught. The national anthem, the "Qaumi Tarana," was almost blistered into our memory. There was an occasion in Lahore when Hafiz Jallundari, the poet, and unfortunately the author of the national anthem, came over for lunch. He was a wizened, kindly little man, and we liked his graciousness, particularly when Khansama the cook brought the *phulkas* in for our meal. We know that our cook had been a poet—he sat and sang poems to himself in the courtyard each afternoon—but I must say I felt somewhat ashamed when he carried in the *rotis*, the bread, for our lunch, and our honored guest Hafiz Sahib stood up to embrace him, saying, "Ilum Din! You wonderful Punjabi poet!" They embraced. "Ilum Din! Why have you been so absent from our *musharias*, our poetry readings?" I felt ashamed. Because he has been too busy cooking our *rotis*, we thought quietly.

That luncheon was fated to end in some disaster. It's your fault, Pip. When we were on our best behavior for two hours straight and our behavior threads were wearing thin, you should not have asked the poet to stand up and sing the national anthem to us. We children dutifully stood up, deserting our green tea and possibly a small dessert of *firni* (rice pudding, but much nicer). As Hafiz Jallundari began to sing that heart-lifting song, his voice quavered as much as his Lucknowi pajamas. One by one we broke into laughter, behaving just as skittles do, for Ifat would pretend to be the bowling ball, nudging Shahid and saying with an assumed frown, "Stop laughing, Shahid"; he would adopt her mode and nudge me, saying, "Stop laughing, Sara," while I had nothing but the infants Tillat and Irfan to tell, "Stop it, stop it, stop it." The latter, however, were so glad to see their elder siblings in such good humor that they pranced about us as though in carnival. And the poet—his eyes closed—continued singing all four of those long stanzas, from the first joyous *shadbad* to the last *Saya-e-Khuda-ya-Zuljilal*. We were chastized quite severely when our guests had left. "Don't you know how rude you were?" Mamma scolded. "What if I were to say Lord Byron came over for tea in Wales and I misbehaved?" "Did he and did you?" I asked, cheekily risking the wrath that inevitably followed.

I am too tired to construct a proper chronology of what constitutes the history of Pakistan. We know that it began suddenly, and that—aside from all the unrecountable slaughter that accompanied the partition of India—a little joke did attend the sundering of the subcontinent. Mountbatten was the last viceroy and doubtless not completely ignorant of the shenanigans his wife was up to. He set the fourteenth of August as the date for the 1947 severance; all seemed in good order, until the Hindu soothsayers approached Nehru to say that the fourteenth was a most inauspicious day; the fifteenth would be far more appropriate. Nehru, an urbane man, was irritated, but far too politic to alienate his constituency. Mountbatten agreed to the day's delay. Jinnah, however, equally urbane, turned stubborn: "You *said* the fourteenth and it will *be* the fourteenth!" he declared, in a miff. As a consequence, Pakistan became independent on the fourteenth of August 1947, and India, on the fifteenth. Aside from the absurdity of such a squabble, it does make one wonder. In what no-man's-land did India reside in those twenty-four hours? Between being the brightest jewel in the Crown and the largest democracy in the world, was it actually allowed—even for a day—to be unnamed, itself? Beloved Eqbal Ahmad traveled in a foot convoy from the Red Fort in Delhi across the precarious borders into Lahore. When they left, their numbers were in the thousands; they arrived a few exhausted hundreds. Eqbal told me one tale of that journey that arrested, startled me: one of the immigrants in that bitterly motley group was named Resham Khan and was clearly an addict of some sorts. He took *charas*, I think (What is *charas*? Is it opium?), and walked bent double, coughing like a hag. But then something happened. A few Sikh soldiers ostensibly accompanying the convoy took to molesting one of the traveling maidens (a belly from Delhi), and Resham suddenly straightened up and took command. His bearing, his posture changed; he moved from being a cripple to a savior. It was Resham who led that ragged and diminished group up to the Lahore Fort, and Eqbal kept telling me how proud he was of that man's transmutation. The travelers dispersed as such convoys do, in a desperate wish for a home, for a bed. Some months later, outside the Pak Tea House in Lahore (a fine establishment where writers gathered), Eqbal noticed a crippled, obviously addicted beggar on the pavement. He bent to drop some *annas* into the begging bowl, and then noticed to his horror that it was Resham Khan. "It was Resham," wept Eqbal. "How could he have done this to himself, how could he, how could he?" I wept with him, a companion in his compassion.

Would Faiz have been at the Pak Tea House? I can't remember whether he was in jail or not at that time. He was imprisoned on some conspiracy charges in the Lahore Fort, an uncomfortable but somewhat poetic place, and he certainly wrote some fine poetry in those quarters. He had a voice that matched his poems, and I recall hearing him read slowly, steadily:

ہم جو تاریک راہوں میں مارے گئے

"Those of us who were killed in darkened streets,"

a poem that I believe was an elegy for the Rosenbergs. You were always generous about his poetry, Pip, even when you did not care for his politics. With me, with all your loved ones, I have listened to you reciting:

مجھ سے پہلی سی محبت مری محبوب نہ مانگ
اور بھی دکھ ہیں زمانے میں محبت کے سوا

"My lover, do not ask for that former love . . .
There are more griefs in these times aside from love."

And sometimes even more quietly to yourself:

کر رہا تھا غم جہاں کا حساب
آج تم یاد بے حساب آئے

"I was counting the griefs of the world.
Today I have remembered you countlessly."

What were you remembering, Pip? Was it us, or was it Mamma? Or
was it Pakistan?

I watched you, Pip, during the bitter war of 1971. It takes me much
time to mention that war because of its colossal failures, its unutterable
consumption of lives. I am not sorry Bangladesh is in place—it was a
stupid idea, anyway, to have an east wing and a west wing of Pakistan,
separated by a thousand-odd miles of enemy territory, like a bird without a body. But continually we had to think about the lives. My friends in
college said, "Well, at least we don't have to spend each autumn making
cyclone relief packages anymore!" It was true. In prior years, each time a
cyclone or a devastating flood hit Bengal, we young girls were required
to give up our free time in college, to sit packing up care bundles to send
to the erstwhile East Pakistan, to the victims of weather's ravages. Scant
care. The packages consisted of a washcloth, aspirin, uncooked lentils,
a small bag of rice. "Where will they find unpolluted water in which to
cook these items," I thought bitterly, "or even in that great preponder-
ance of liquid a body pure enough to rinse their cloths?" Think of the
grotesque bounty of similar packages, rained on Afghanistan, rained on
Iraq. Ilyas, Nuzzi's cook, was from Bengal and to this day is still with our
sweet brother-in-law Feroze. Ilyas told me that the last time he returned
to Bangladesh there was another enormous upheaval in the Ganges,
uprooting villages, wreaking havoc where havoc should not have been
wreaked. He said that he and his family spent days clinging to some
trees: how is it possible to live for a week in the desperate embrace of
a tree? I felt ashamed. But Ilyas was back in Karachi, with his family
alive and well. And then he touchingly asked me to send him a watch
from America: "latest model, latest model," he kept repeating, as though
watches like automobiles renew themselves each year. I am glad to say

I found him the most gaudy, gadget-ridden specimen that could be located in Abu Dhabi's duty-free airport (Abu Dhabi, duty-free capital of the world) on my next trip to Karachi. And when I handed Ilyas his gift, what a smile lit up his eyes.

Ilyas called my niece Laila "Baby." We did have fun together. She laughed so much when, after Nuzzi's funeral, I muttered, "I feel like tucking Baby into my armpit and taking her home with me." Nuz had a wonderful pebblelike laugh, and Laila has somehow replicated it: clatter, clatter, clatter, Nuz used to laugh, and mini-clatter, mini-clatter, mini-clatter, laughs my niece. She knows Karachi all too well, with its traffic and its charms. I don't know if she would remember Mr. Liaquat Ali or Khwaja Nazimuddin, the latter a relative of my dearest friend, Nuzhat Ahmad. How is it, when I am primed to write about Pakistan politics, that such a strong urge takes me to write about my loved ones instead? Nuzhat Ahmad is such an urge.

I miss her when she is off in Kosovo. And her mother, I miss her too, the only woman I could call—without the least affectedness—Aunty. Aunty loved me. She cooked her wonderful food, froze it, and then sent it express mail to Bloomington, Indiana, from Washington, D.C. She had no idea of the look on the mailman's face when he carried up to my apartment a package dripping not just with water, but with spices and with a watery ghee (clarified butter). The mailman looked pained. But Bilquis Aunty, Nuzhat's mother, had no idea. Neither did she have an inkling about why I was in D.C. some time later, cavorting off with Pathar Nadi. He was there for a conference—events to which I am increasingly allergic—so I would spend the day with Nuzhat Ahmad and then go trotting back of an evening to spend the night with Pathar Nadi. And my sweet aunty, without a glimmer of suspicion in her voice, would look up with such affection: "My poor Sara," she said tenderly, "why do these conferences run from evening to morning? No wonder you look so tired!"

And, Pip, how you admired Nuzhat's father, the only person I call Uncle. He, as a Bengali senior government official, was put in the greatest straits once East Pakistan became Bangladesh. I do not have the time to record the striations of betrayal he faced, when he chose to continue being Pakistani. "Uncle, you must write your story," I urge. "It is history." It is. When I ask him about his decision, he responds, "I was a great believer in Pakistan." He knew how much the Bengalis had contributed to the independence movement and hoped—sad optimist that he is—that regional disputes, territorial squabbles, would somehow resolve themselves. They didn't. Right now the division between provinces in Pakistan is about as rigid as the language differences that tear the land into bitternesses of supremacy. But my uncle remains constant. He lives—in the tragic loss of his wonderful companion—as a committed citizen of the old idea of pre-1970 Pakistan, in Bethesda, Maryland.

It is hard for me to raise the issue of the huge travails that created Bangladesh. The war should not be mentioned, since it killed so much, and the two-nation theory was the least of its casualties. I can only smile wryly when people tell me that I have no right to talk with any authority about Pakistan, since I have been gone for so many decades. "I do not wish to be an author," I reply. And somehow it brings to mind your fourth book, Pip, called *Pakistan's Lost Years*. How many more years have been lost, since you conceived of that title? I dare not mention Kashmir and the futilities it has accrued nor the disputed waterways of far more value than beauty. Is Pakistan becoming a synonym for death? Perhaps so, Pip. We have known much death in our family.

Of all your children, Pip, I surmise Ifat was the most Pakistani. I don't know if she was cognizant of as much of its history as was Shahid, but she certainly entered its spirit with an indomitable aplomb. She loved to watch polo—a game invented in the northwest province of the subcontinent, of course—and was also moved by tent pegging. *Neza-bazi*: a truly beautiful game, I must confess. It involves horses and riders, and little stakes stuck in the field. The riders have spears; they gallop up at ferocious speed, crying, *"Ya Ali madad!"* "Oh, Ali, give me help!" (Ali was a close relative of Muhammad's [peace], you see.) If at that pace they manage to prong a wooden stake, they lift it up in triumph over their heads, and then the stake unfurls a stream of silk fabric, a slender and fluttering banner of victory. It is quite a delight to watch. For one thing, it involves no carnage of any kind; the horses seem to enjoy it, and even when a stake is missed, the rider does not retire in any ignominious fashion. Rather, be-turbanned as he is, he canters off proudly as though the field had been at fault and he none other than a defeated hero.

You did love Ifat, Pip, perhaps more than any of your children. That is hardly a surprise, and I think it had little to do with Pakistan. No. Remember her living face with something of the joy that I bestow upon my friends when I recite, repeatedly:

"The dazzle of the sea, my darling."

It is a forgotten MacNeice poem, a fugue, and I fondly imagine that my continued recitation of it has something to do with its survival. It ends with lines that have Ifat's name written on them:

But you are alive without question,
Like the dazzle of the sea, my darling.

Pip was so lost when Ifat was killed. I imagine that it was wrenchingly easier for him to see Pakistan—his prime love—dismantled, rather than his daughter. I begged him to be at peace, to remember that the country still continued. But his grief, like so much about him, was adamant. "Do you know how straight she stood?" Pip demanded of me, as though I were a being in remiss. Yes, I knew, for she bewitched me, with the skull of a leopard and the manner of a hawk. I even thought Maud Gonne must have been her sister rather than I was, when I read Yeats's wonder: "Pallas Athene in that straight back and arrogant head." We did not move in our mourning. But even you, Pip, even you, had to laugh when you recalled Ifat in erect attention, singing:

"Long live, you purest land!"

Of course it would live on without her; Pakistan can do without any number of us, pure or impure. We should not even take its name in vain. Yet you did, Pip, and I am still haunted by your manner of expression, your look—even in grief—of astonishment. Even today I wish to take your hand and kiss it in reassurance, saying Pakistan thus far is shoddily and dubiously intact, except that I know you would shake me off impatiently with a gesture that declared my concern was not necessary. It is a necessity for me, however, for how I long to be able to give you what I attempted to give to my sister: "Pallas Athene in that straight back and arrogant head."

The point of the tongue

Pardon that for a barren passion's sake,
Although I have come close on forty-nine,
I have no child, I have nothing but a book,
Nothing but that to prove your blood and mine.

— Y E A T S

I really am close on forty-nine. And I really am close to forgetfulness as well, for they tell me that my brain can no longer sustain another injury: it always was a walnut, anyway, held tightly in a hand that was hot enough. We worried about you, Pip, even as we said that age could not wither you, nor custom stale your infinite variety. They call you illustrious, along with several other nasty names, and I have no idea what effect they have upon your bones, for you were always hurt easily, and often.

It probably didn't trouble you at all, the fact that I had no children: the rest of my siblings were pretty good at that activity, and I'll wager a guess that you could not even count how many grandchildren came your way, let alone great-grandchildren.

A silly tale: visiting Lahore one summer, I was frightened that I might have conceived, so Tillat and I went with great trepidation to a clinic. We must have lied about my name, for unmarried women are not supposed to be in any need of a pregnancy test in Pakistan. We sat waiting, and even my bladder felt disconsolate. Then at last the physician's assistant showed his face to tell us, sadly and compassionately, that the test was negative. Tillat and I were hugging each other with relief, but the assistant took that as a sign of sorrow. He kept regarding me with compassion and—although he didn't actually say so—"better luck next time" was in his eyes. A silly tale.

Luckily, that luck did not come my way. To abort in Pakistan—an overaborted country—would have been quite messy, coat hangers and all, unless I put myself in the care of the local midwife and her sorcerer's fingers. She was something remarkable, arriving with nothing other than a bottle of bitter oils and her expert fingers. I wonder if such people, straight out of folklore, are better doctors than those who spend years and years in schools of medicine. Here I am quick to exempt you, Dr. Azra Raza, you and your medically minded clan. You and your sisters bring radiance to whatever you do and convert oncology itself into a form of poetry. I will not forget the sight of your six-year-old daughter, Shehr, reciting *ghazal* after *ghazal*, poem after poem, with such enthusiastic confidence. Her face was charming, but something in her expression reminded me of Mīrzā Ghālib, the past master poet of Delhi. There could be no greater compliment, and part of the credit has to go to her mother, my friend. We met by accident—through my writing, in fact—but since that time have behaved as though we were childhood comrades. The Raza clan, my salaams to you.

Perhaps I should have taken the time to read you some of my poems in a formal fashion, Pip, because, indifferent though they are, they were always on my tongue and became in a certain way the point of the tongue. You, however, would have become suspicious, translating the great excuse of poetic license into one of your hard-core facts. What would you have made, for example, of the following fragment, which reads:

> No, sir, say no.
> This night keep your knighthood,
> Wear my virtue if you will:
> I have no use for it. But still,
> For the sake of restfulness, say no.
> Let my legs, my arms be instruments,
> Not surfaces to suffer your touch.
> And just before you sleep beneath the stars
> Think quietly
> On the magnificent irrelevance of beauty.

No, my dear, my Pip, I could not have read that to you, for just consider all the directions into which it would have sent your mind racing. Certain acts—such as writing a poem—are best obliterated, consigned to the sweeter sleep of forgetfulness.

While on the subject of irrelevant beauty, how astounded Pip always was to observe Tillat, always so artlessly beautiful. (You have to lose your braces and your blubber, Tat: on that I insist.) How her name has become part of our household machinery in Maine! The story is convoluted. During our girlhood, I would frequently call Tillat "Tattycoram," that most peculiar character in *Little Dorrit*, who, when on the verge of losing her temper, was told: "Count to ten." My sister is not given to fits and starts as am I, but it seemed like a good appellation for her, anyway. "Tillat" is not an easy one to nick into a name, and I could hardly repeat the excellence of Nuzzi's refrain when she bounced the infant Tillat on her knee:

> Tillaty-tu
> Poppety-chou
> How do you do?
> I love you!

Tillat adored this adventure, as did my observant father, so gradually the term "poppety-chou" entered our vocabulary as a synonym for a ravishing charm. Nuz was taking evening classes in French while we were in London: does that explain the "chou," I wonder. The baby's lingo turned Tillat to "illa," which was sweet, except that Pip was very affronted when we siblings naturally turned it into *"illa billa hu."* It wasn't the blasphemy that was so offensive; it was the notion that his darling illa could also be "billa": a tomcat, a rhyme certainly of the wrong gender.

In any case, when Tillat and her family were visiting Maine some years ago, my husband looked at her most genially, saying, "Tillat is such a pretty name! I'm going to call my next dog Tillat!" The expression on her face did not suggest she was particularly flattered. It took me back to Lahore, when young Shahid made the mistake of telling Pip, "Papa, we thought we heard you calling us, but in fact it was a dog barking!" Ifat and I would never have repeated that little joke to our father, and quite rightly so. He bristled with umbrage, and Shahid was in Coventry for some days. In a similar fashion, Tillat did not look amused when Austin bestowed his compliment on her, although she was too polite to say so. And after our dog Deenie died, when we acquired the most remarkable little Sealyham terrier, I was horrified to note that Austin had remembered his proposition. I said, "Let's call her Tattycoram; it's so much easier to pronounce than Tillat! Furthermore, she looks just like a Tatty!" At first I think Tillat was somewhat possessive of her endearment and resented it being bestowed on anyone else, even though the original came from Dickens. On her most recent trip, however, as she watched Tatty racing round the house on one of her inexplicable marathon runs, Tillat agreed that the dog was born to be called Tatty. I would stand in the kitchen and shout out, "Tat? Tat?" And when both of them came running, how happy I would feel.

Now we must return to Lahore, all of us together, to the summer evenings that engendered so many of these little tales. It is surprising to me to recollect how few evenings we were all there together, although those dew-filled nights boasted of such festivity. Yes, we were festive when in one another's company, a fact that I think registered as an irritant to my siblings' various mates: it possibly still does. No matter that the latters should be perplexed, taken aback, when a perfectly reasonable evening should be interrupted by the sudden growl from Pip, "Get out of my sight." We complied without a comment, and I must confess that I became the most frequent recipient of Pip's command when I was on the verge of leaving Pakistan and obeying him most literally. Recently, I gave Tillat quite a few laughters when I read to her a newspaper article that described me as humble, polite, and accessible. She conceded to the "polite," but the other adjectives my sister dismissed forthwith. "Humble and accessible? *You? No!* You are cold and proud." I feel perfectly contented with those epithets: they are becoming, in their own way, and in perfect synchronicity with the times when I looked upon my family in a Lahore garden to utter to myself:

مدّت ہوئی ہے یار کو مہماں کیے ہوئے
جوشِ قدح سے بزم چراغاں کیے ہوئے
غالب

It has been centuries since my friend was my guest,
when with language alone, we have lit candles through the night.

— GHĀLIB

After you had left, Pip, stepsister Shahida began pestering each of us for a "por-torni." I am good at deciphering Urdu accents, but this phrase flummoxed me. It was only after some legalese was dispatched to us—specifically to Shahid's wife, Jane, the lawyer—that I realized "por-torni" equals "power of attorney." How stupid of me not to have made the connection. We did not really have any objections to giving Shahida control over Pip's estate, as it was grandiloquently called: there are some pictures that I miss, some china, but they belong elsewhere, to a different era. I had met up with Austin in Boston, and he, when I showed him the document, insisted that I get it notarized then and there and put it in the mail at once. Austin is like that—sensible. He also knows my tendency to prevaricate, to put things so irredeemably beyond a deadline that deadlines do not matter anymore. It's true. But for his urging, "por-torni" would in all likelihood be still about my person. So we went to the Paki Honorary Consul General's office, who exclaimed to me, "I did not know your father had died!" I cannot tell you how it stops my soul, Pip, when I hear that simple past tense and have to reply quietly, "Yes." ("Why should a dog, a horse, a rat, have life, / And thou no breath at all? Thou'lt come no more, / Never, never, never, never, never!") The consul was full of condolence, saying what a great human being my father was, what a wonderful human being. Then he added—as though reality had hit him—"and a most irascible man!"

I liked that phrase. It gave me pleasing visions of Pip in Boston tormenting the consul when long-distance phone lines to Pakistan were not working, or when a car had not arrived on time. Yes, he could be irascible. There was one occasion when he had been summoned to Islamabad to see the president—I cannot remember who was in power—and thought he was late for his flight. Unfortunately, there was a plane on the runway just ready to taxi off. Pip pushed past the astonished security guards like a wild bull, mounted the pilot's ladder, and threw himself into the copilot's seat, to the considerable bewilderment of the crew. "Take me to Islamabad!" "But, sir," the pilot said gently, "this is a cargo plane. We are taking a shipment of bananas to Saudi Arabia." Pip looked around and, yes, they were right. No passengers at all, but plenty of bananas. So Pip dismounted and, to the greater surprise of the security guards, did not appear to be in the least embarrassed: instead, he was chortling at his own mistake and silenced them with a cheery wave, accompanied by a jovial cry, "I'm not a banana!"

"Irascible" is even a mild word for such behavior. There was a time when my parents went to innumerable diplomatic parties: my mother quite disliked it, for she would probably prefer to be sitting at home reading Elizabeth Bowen or Maynard Mack. When I met Maynard at Yale, I felt constrained to tell him that my mother had been his student once and considered him one of the finest critics she had read. "What a highly intelligent woman your mother must have been!" Maynard exclaimed. She was. And so she felt a trifle pained to be trotted out to so many diplomatic events, particularly since she had to keep one guarded eye over her husband. He could be irascible. Once, when some foreigner was asking Pip about a delicate issue, such as India or Kashmir, my father tried to offset the issue in as reasonable a way as possible. The unsuspecting foreigner did not know better and kept repeating, "But you haven't answered my question." He did not know how explosive was Pip's ire. "Does this man call himself a diplomat?" thundered Pip, and the British ambassador's home froze into silence. This man, confined to the third person, was quite cowed; Pip, with noble scorn about his lips, thundered again: "Does this man call himself a diplomat?"

Pip used to love to read, and one of the poignancies for us to watch was how his increasing ailments robbed him of his favorite habit. In fact, one of my abiding familial memories involves sitting in a living room, each of us absorbed in a different book. We would interrupt one another, too, reading out passages or jokes that really were not relevant to whatever other texts were in our hands. Still, we enjoyed that communal sharing, and then would return to our books. It made us heave a deep sign of patience, however, when Pip took up a novel by P. G. Wodehouse and had to convey his merriment orally, sentence by sentence, line by line. He laughed as heartily as he would over his own jokes: "Bertie Wooster," he exclaimed, "woke up not feeling disgruntled, but not exactly gruntled, either!" It presents a strange picture to the mind's eye: our living room, with Mamma reading endless student exams; Tillat reading D. H. Lawrence; Shahid deep into some history of the Second World War; me perusing Wallace Stevens; and Pip—in one of his rare moments of leisure—engrossed in P. G. Wodehouse. He sat there in fits of laughter, while above him so incongruous hung in all dignity the picture of Pip with Jinnah, both of them looking so statesmanlike.

My father would be pleased to know that Bapsi Sidhwa has become such a close friend of mine, for he admired her work, particularly *Cracking India*. It gave him an uneasy consciousness of the untold deaths partition had entailed, with slaughter of a kind I do not wish to remember or describe. What was he to do in 1947, proudly raising the Pakistani flag in London, with the great distraction of my mother at his side? He thought he was, but he wasn't really, concentrating his gaze on the great falling apart of the Indian subcontinent. Something in the British press failed to convey the helplessness of those people, when trainload after trainload—on both sides of the newly founded borders—arrived with nothing but the dead. I do not mean to be critical of Pip: after all, I was never born a colonized person and do not really know the elation that he felt when he hoisted up the Pakistani flag in London. The flag is a deep green, with a crescent and star at its center, both in white. It also has a white strip down its right side, to indicate that while the majority of Pakistan's population was Muslim (green), the country still welcomed minorities (white), as well. Has that strip been taken away today, I wonder.

When I first came to America, I was nonplussed to see how many houses flew the American flag on their front lawns. It is certainly not a common habit in England, nor in the part of the world from where I hail. We basically use them on government buildings or semiofficial residences. One fourteenth of August Pakistan Day, however, Pip in a fit of patriotism decided we should fly a flag on the roof of our house. Shortly thereafter the cook, the bearer, and the driver came in with their greetings: "*Mubarik, mubarik!* Congratulations Sahib! [my Pip]. Sahib has become a minister!" The government in power was one with which Pip was in variance and I believe had jailed him once or twice. The notion that he could be a minister of theirs caused him considerable disgust, and he ordered the flag to be taken down forthwith. "Why, Papa?" I asked. "It looks so pretty fluttering up there!" He burst into laughter, took me by my four-year-old shoulders, and said, "You'll understand someday."

Maybe I do understand, Pip, but it has taken a long time coming. I do not understand why the country you loved so passionately—some of it has rubbed off on your children, too—did not take the time to recognize you for what you were: passionate, preposterous. I was frozen in the weeks while I was waiting for Pip's death: when it came, the waiting did not matter, for I was still in profound surprise. "Didn't Wordsworth write a poem, 'We Are Seven'?" Pip asked me with a sob in his eyes shortly after Ifat died. "Yes, he did," I answered, dry-eyed. After my father decided to die, there were some harebrained schemes of seeing that he should be buried next to Jinnah, in Karachi. If he were alive, he would probably be gratified by that proposal, but since he is not, let his bones rest in Lahore, in some proximity to his wife and to his daughter. I will go there, I hope in the company of Tillat or her family, in order that I may feel—with courtesy—less alone.

I write with the light failing and not a breath of air among the leaves. You would have approved of this coastline, Pip, for you were always moved to be poetical when close to water. I will take you here someday and plant you among the rue that I will wear with a difference. Would a monument embarrass you or perhaps my siblings, making them say behind my back, "This time, she has gone too far"? I imagine it reading something along the lines of "father foresaken, forgive your son," or perhaps a stern admonition:

کئی ہے رات ہنگامہ گستری میں تری
سحر قریب ہے، اللہ کا نام لے ساقی!
اقبال

You have spent your night in the noise of passion.
Dawn comes; take Allah's name, winebearer!

—I Q B Ā L

When you are irritable at such a plan and say, "Get out of my sight," as is your wont, then I will surely obey. Will I, however, let you out of my sight, much as the birds that flutter with such special providence? No, I will absent me from felicity awhile to tell your stories, and if, my father, you think that you could leave such hollows about my eyes, then you must hear my repetition: "Never, never, never, never, never."

Good night, sweet Pip, flights of angels sing thee to thy rest! You will be back more times than you know. I was always obstinate.